# I Hate Black People Who Hate Black People

*A Grassroots Analysis of an untreated disease
In the African American community*

David Hunter

ISBN-10: 1463717350

ISBN-13: 978-1463717353

# Dedication

To my family and friends

# CONTENTS

## INTRODUCTION

## CHAPTER

# I HATE BLACK PEOPLE WHO HATE BLACK PEOPLE

## INTRODUCTION

I would have argued that hell itself was home to nothing more ungodly and hideous than white supremacy has been in my mind over the years. So powerful has been my aversion to this disease of the human spirit that it has caused me to spend the greater part of my life trying to avoid situations, circumstances, and even opportunities that might personally expose me, in small or large measure, to its Caucasian carriers. Open and subtle expressions alike of their bigotry exploded emotions in me that I sometimes experienced difficulty containing. Then one day I saw clearly for the first time, something I had been only looking at all my life. It suddenly dawned on me that while I was despising, ducking, dodging, and denouncing anti-blackness of the Caucasoid kind, I had all the while been couched in the bosom of a beast ten times more malignant and a thousand times uglier: anti-blackness of the African American kind, white supremacy's hate-child. White Supremacy paled by comparison. I looked up and there stood a whole "new" group of racists, looking down on the Black race, stereotyping it, and hating its phenotype. Here was an unlabeled breed of extremists and other individuals, black themselves, but hating Black people or having a low opinion of people of African descent.

If this was an epiphany it was not the realization of Black self-hate/disrespect as a new reality, but rather my weighing it as the more obstructive and, at the same time, less resisted, of two unwelcome forces in our lives. Even worse I saw this paradox being seen as a common cold instead of the cancerous malignancy that it is. While we have dutifully decried blatant expressions of white bigotry, Black self-hate practically dances before us, butt-naked in the streets without shame, inspiring only laughter, if anything at all. It has lain there undisturbed, at the root of many of our problems and the main source of our remedial anemia. Although some of our leaders, writers and historians have responsibly denounced the phenomenon, it has never really inspired the clarion call it has long deserved.

I am not on a high horse, because up to the point

of my "epiphany", virtually all Black anti-Blackness was overwhelmingly represented in my thoughts by the "Uncle Tom" prototype. But the attitudes I wish to call attention to deserve distinction from the cowardly Uncle Tom mentality.

The object of my analysis is a demonic group of African Americans who chronically slander Black nature without mercy.

It is without a scintilla of reservation, that I sing my sad song to the world: I hate Black people who hate Black people. I am sorry but they are to me every bit as contemptible as *white* people who hate Black people and even more problematic. Please join me in counting them among the lowest creatures in all creation. I rank them in worth somewhere between a cockroach and a cocker spaniel.

I have good reason for feeling the way I feel. Their anti-black thought patterns combine with other anti-Black attitudes of lesser intensity to form the basis of what is, by leaps and bounds, the greatest single problem Black people have ever faced.

They stand between a Black America who needs much more of itself and a
Black America that gives a sufficient fraction of its dormant powers.

Who needs the Ku Klux Klan with them around? There are more than enough Black on Black racists saying and doing more anti-black things in a single day than some white supremacists do in a lifetime. At least the European who is openly hostile to blackness gets sanctioned by his peers and others, however sanctimonious such censorship may be. These individuals don't even as much as get branded "racist". Yet that is exactly what they are when it comes to Black people if you go by the things they say and do. Are they not evolutionary oddballs? What other species from Adam to atom-splitting has ever hated its own kind.

Some of the extreme ones (I call them SAMBOITES) can be heard blaspheming blackness as if they were card-carrying members of another racial group. (Oddly enough, if someone of another racial group uttered in their presence the exact same anti-black phrases they air themselves, even they would get mad.)

The idea of Black inferiority is granted a whole new dimension of validity when it is echoed by members of the very group being looked down upon. The very ideas, half-truths, myths, and falsehoods that we have wished for so long to disappear from white minds forever are alive and well in a sizable number of black minds. Their beliefs are not just sitting there looking ugly. They are at work in our lives, decimating our powers and dehumanizing us as did and as does their progenitor, white supremacy. With their perverted assistance, the Black community is depriving itself and the rest of the world of an enormous reservoir of creative aptitude lying dormant under thick layers of self-doubt and a bevy of non-clinical complexes. These complexes affect even the emotional development of our children. We have developed the bad habit of building self-worth around net worth, which is always dangerous but even more so when you're broke. Almost everything if not everything that is comparatively wrong with Black America can be traced to Black self-hate and its original sponsor, white supremacy. Just as kryptonite, a piece of his home planet, Krypton, drains power from the fictional superman, false ideas about our home continent, Africa have drained and weakened us psychologically. Superman ultimately realized that he had to steer clear of fragments of the very soil on which he was born. In our supreme ignorance of Africa and its splendid history, many of us have done the same. Africa has been our Kryptonite, when it should have been spiritual protein. Mother Africa and its spectacular history has always been a great source of spiritual momentum for me as well as immaculate certification of the comparative worth of African people.

But, like it or not, at no fault of my own, there are Black people on this planet who feel just the opposite and there are others whose mind house a range of milder but still harmful ideas about the Black race.

I refer to the ones who have any discernible measure of self-hate/dislike as "Blackteria". The "Blackteria" are further subdivided into three groups depending upon their degree of dislike for Blackness. Unfortunately, you don't have to wait on the circus to come to town to see one. They are not rare. One might be your neighbor, your blood kin, someone you consider a friend, or God forbid, the man or woman you see in the mirror. As surreal as all this may seem to some, there is indeed here in America and other places in our world, a wide range of mild to militant anti-Black sentiments prevalent in black people themselves, and the situation needs to be addressed with a much greater sense of urgency.     There are despicable patterns of thought that need to be chased, challenged, and ultimately changed. While this has been known on some scale for a long time, we have never really treated this malady I call the **Sambo Virus**, in proportion to the damage it does or the intra-racial love it inhibits. Without hesitation, I would trade in the whole civil rights movement for a movement of equal intellectual vigor and bravado against our underestimated self-disrespect and self-hate.

The anti-black ideas spawned by the Sambo Virus are not just inert mental data or idle thoughts. They affect interpersonal relationships, even ones as natural and delicate as mother and child. They cause us to stereotype each other and discriminate against our own with what little power we have to do so.

Perhaps the most harmful effect of the virus and white supremacy has been against our confidence, as individuals and as a group. I have always suspected that confidence is grossly underrated in measurements of competence.

Confidence is much more than just some handy little spectacle in the human personality. It is instead the escape velocity of all human potential. In other words, its absence or preservation should never be taken lightly. Confidence can and has been the difference between a George Washington Carver who makes 300 products from a peanut and a savant of equal aptitude who winds up working for peanuts.

Hence, I am not advocating Black on Black love and respect for militant or spiteful reasons.

The recovery of Black self-love is vital to our well-being and maybe even our survival. If I thought it was one iota less critical to our lives, I would sit back in silence as do many *guilty* by-standers. An extreme antipathy toward Black self-hate and self-dislike must be cultivated in the Black community. Their untreated existence has helped paralyzed our natural abilities to foster sound human development in a world that has tried to lower our humanity. Childrearing, for example, has sunken to an all-time low in many areas, causing us to recycle a more anti-communal crop with each new generation.

Being manufactured are twisted, self-centered, egomaniacal monsters who have all but cast aside their natural sensibilities in order to manage an image or assuage personal pain and self-doubt.

Those infected with the **Sambo virus** probably don't realize that they help guarantee our elusive quest for social and economic equality will remain a pipe dream for a long time if not forever. Just sit back and take notice and you will see what I, myself, have tried to deny for many years. We have been pitted against not just one, but two anti- Black groups, as if white racism by itself wasn't dreadful enough. Our very own anti-black beliefs have worked against us, heavily taxing our communal values, our childrearing, our family values, and our friendships. As long as we as a group harbor the beliefs we harbor, we will never give ourselves to ourselves the way we gave ourselves to the world at the dawn of civilization.

As it is we have a surplus of small spirits who are desperately egocentric, and just as likely to be found behind pulpits as they are behind bars.

I want to see this change because I love my family and because I feel deep sympathy and love for the Black family as a whole. Somehow I know that their incarceration, their mental anguish, their heart disease, their poverty, their starvation, their criminal records, and almost all the pain they feel, in a chaos theory sort of way and even more direct way, has something to do with their exposure to Black and White Negrophobia.

Here in the American south, I sometimes feel like I live in a sea of self-hate.

In all modesty, I consider myself the exact opposite of the most extreme Samboite. I see myself as a swan living among swans who think of themselves ugly ducklings.

Why is it, I ask, we get all worked up when whites make open racist statements about black people, yet respond like zombies, if at all, when the same or similar statements are made by black people about black people. Where is it written that it's okay for Black people themselves to degrade the Black race?

It should bother us more when anti-black statements come from the mouths of Black individuals because they signify patterns of thought that paralyze our chance for bringing about the high level of intra-racial cooperation necessary to give us a fighting chance against our troubles. No real success will come otherwise. Anyone who believes we can ever rise from the depths of our dystopian despair without first building a stronger intra-racial bond is daydreaming, drunk, delusional, or just plain dumb. Without moving toward what I define as **Kemet Kemistry**, or strong self love and support, the only rise we will ever see is a rise in the number of cases of high blood pressure and heart disease. This is not to say that I would not want to live in a multi-cultural, color-blind society that is truly just. I believe firmly that all Black Americans share or have shared some version of Martin Luther King's famous dream. But it has always seemed to me a bit Pollyannaish to wait on others to change. Black people need each other's love and support whether people of European decent love us, hate us, or anything in between. We need much greater communal health which means we need a strong antiseptic response to the spiritual virus and germs I hope to help magnify by this work. If we are to have any chance of solving our gargantuan slate problems, black self-hate or the Sambo Virus must become monumentally repulsive in our minds the way white racism was in our minds during the so called Jim Crow era. Black self hate must become vividly visible, studied, targeted, and slain; else we will go on begging lifetime after lifetime. In our current state of affairs we are like turtles crossing the highway, creatures among which there is no lore or angst that speaks to the dangers of being crushed by motor vehicles. Yet turtles die all the time trying to get to the other side of the road. This is how I see us as a group seeing self-hatred/self-disrespect. We see it but we don't see it. Its invisibility renders it lethal.

Something must be done about the villains who inspired the words of this work. Something must be done about the atmosphere that breeds their way of thinking. Some things must be added to it and some things must be taken away. Some number of us must find and exercise the manhood to confront *that* and *those* we know to be wrong, be it a popular belief or tradition, a materialistic evangelist, a lying history book, or the devil himself. No one, absolutely no one, should tell us how to do battle.

We must pay particular attention to bad interpretations of holy writ which keep us from acting in concert for the common good of people with common problems and common vulnerability.

I dream of the day we begin to employ real manhood to fight our own anti-black thought patterns the way we fought race discrimination in the fifties and sixties. There we fought bravely and skillfully for respect and free participation in America's socioeconomic scheme. Yet we have collectively failed to feel the life force being drained from us by the mythology, half-truths, and outright falsehoods that form the basis of the self-hate paradox.

I, for one, am more than willing to go to my grave being despised doing what I know to be right. I have no appetite whatsoever to be accepted by anyone for doing what is popular or traditional, but still wrong.

So many of the black minds housing the toxins I have referenced thus far have no idea whatsoever that we and the rest of the people of this world are sustained today by the technological ingenuity passed down by our black ancestry.

What technological and moral darkness this world might be in had it not been for the darkness that inspires shame in too many Black people! Therefore, I feel no guilt whatsoever declaring my hatred for black people who hate black people. I am convinced it is their unchallenged power that keeps us down, more than any other single force today.

I vehemently reject the idea that the *practice* of today's white supremacy has ever been clever enough to keep us down this long by itself. It needed our help. White supremacy as an idea, is, and always has been, our greatest enemy. The very belief in Black inferiority holds us back the way a flimsy rope can restrain a full grown elephant, despite its great strength. Willie Lynch's formula for keeping slaves divided is not the reason for our present day Samboism. We have not, contrary to what many believe, been systematically tricked into thinking the way many of us think. Our present day dysfunction is more of a natural consequence of being severed from the continuum and certitudes that other groups take for granted. This rendered and still renders us highly vulnerable to the weak and strong signals broadcasted by white supremacy. Other groups are not as much unified as they are simply undivided. But, thank God for this much: It just so happens that the roots of the broken Continuum from which we sprang is second to none in might or morality. Of this I am sure. But I am still very worried that if we don't wake up to our self-hate, we will all one day wake up extinct.

The most unmanageable, most untamable wild animal in all creation is the human mind. Much of what people think is guided by emotional preferences, fear, ignorance or any combination of the three. This is why I believe our African ancestors found it so important to stress, "Man Know Thyself" (Eurocentric historians give credit to Socrates for this idea). At this point in history, we are the underdogs.

The brain is the human being's best weapon against anything. That weapon must be refined and cultivated in order to achieve maximum output. It cannot be diseased by self-doubt, paranoia, vanity, fear, or ignorance. Unfortunately this is the crippling condition that besets so many minds in general, but we, least of all, can afford the handicap.

This, therefore, is a call to warfare; intellectual warfare, against Black self-haters, self-dislikers and all variation of such thought patterns that contribute to this paralysis. Those of us who flunked the school of self-hatred and the most slanderous course of its curriculum, "**his-story**", must arm ourselves with more truth and courage, in order to neutralize the influence of those who dislike, despise, or disrespect blackness. It is hoped that this work makes a contribution to that end.

## CHAPTER I
## THE BLACKTERIA

The thought patterns of the people who inspired this book are toxic to our spiritual recovery, which is in turn a prerequisite to our ability to effectively address the problems that plague the Black community. They therefore deserve a name and a description which makes them easier targets for Afrocentric proselytizers. The present namelessness of these varying attitudes leaves them untamable by the type of spontaneous sanctions that tend to inhibit or at least send underground "Uncle Tom" type behavior, to cite one example.

The very existence of such words helps keep certain impulses in check.

The categories referenced in this chapter represent some of the most trenchant attitudes or thought patterns occurring in Black minds about the Black race.

The categories probably won't encompass all Black attitudes toward Blackness nor should they be considered absolute. Some overlap each other.

Some individuals may not fit cleanly in either group, which may or may not be good.

See which one best describes you, your best friend, or anyone else in your personal circle when it comes to attitude toward Black people as a group and their struggle. All of us who know better should be about the business of converting members of the undesirable groups into self-lovers. We make the Black community and the world a better place with each conversion. Labeling attitudes with these names might be effective because some people try to live down undesirable reputations by staging attitudes and actions that contrast what they think people think of them. This may prove healthy because even fake pro-Black opinions can contribute to our spiritual healing.

**The Malcolm Vacuums**

The greatest number of all **Blackteria** probably falls near the milder end of the self-hate spectrum. I call them "**Malcolm Vacuums** "because of the absence in their minds of any significant consciousness about the black struggle. "Malcolm Vacuums" are apt to commit what might be considered misdemeanors from time to time such as referring to curly or straight hair on Black heads as "good hair". Such utterances may seem harmless to the users but they add up to do harm that we ultimately feel and see. Most **Malcolm Vacuums** are anti-black by default. In other words, a position of neutrality and silence serves the cause of the **Ebony Ebb**, or the general decline of the quality of Black life.

Most of them have little to no consciousness of the intellectual resistance of white supremacy. It is more accurate to say the **Malcolm Vacuums** "hate on" blackness than to say they hate Black people. They are more or less victims of innocent ignorance than anything, but their anti-black thought patterns are still problematic. Malcolm Vacuums tend to buy into the Black stereotypes hook, line, and sinker. Many of them have very limited general knowledge. Most of them say and do anti-black things out of sheer ignorance. Most of them think Africa is a great big jungle. I don't hate Malcolm Vacuums. In fact I find some of them even loveable when they are "off duty" from voicing their myth-ridden opinions about Blackness. But when they *are* on duty, they scare me to death.

### The UnBlacks

Clustered around the middle of the spectrum is the bunch that commits the same type crimes as Malcolm Vacuums and more. They are guilty most of neglecting the common good of Black people. They give little or no analytical thought to the horrible conditions besetting great numbers of Black people. Their consciousness of blackness ebbs and flows, with adversarial moments. Many of them shy away from conversations about race and race issues. Many are almost totally disinterested in the subject. They dignify their disinterest with cosmetic claims. The black church is their favorite hang out and hiding place. Ironically, the moral messages of the New Testament are foreign, irrelevant and academic to them. Religious hypocrisy is a way of life for many in this group. A high percentage of them think Africa is a jungle, despite the fact that many are college graduates. They do not see themselves having any role or responsibility of any size for fighting the "Ebony Ebb". Only sensational cases like the O. J. trial and verdict or the Rodney King beating wake them up for a few days, after which they fall back to sleep.

They are subject to walk right past a black-owned business 50 yards from where they live to get to a non black business 50 miles down the road. White ice is indeed colder than black ice to them. I call members of this group the **UNBLACKS.**

I find the overwhelming majority of the ones I have met to be boring and predictable automatons. There are few things I dread more than being forced into a polite conversation with one.

**The Samboite**

Toward the extreme end of the self-hate spectrum is the type I consider militantly anti-black, although not necessarily openly vitriolic. I call members of this group **Samboites.** Their intellectual make up comprises nearly all the aspects of the first two groups and more. **Samboites** would serve our cause best if they were snatched up tonight by intergalactic explorers and transported to another star system, never to be heard from again.

Damn them to hell, this third group. If anybody ever deserved to be discriminated against, it is this bunch. **Samboites** deserve whatever contempt and scorn you can generate toward them. We waste too much antipathy on klansmen and loose-mouthed talk-show hosts. Save some for these detestable demons.

They have inherited the mantle of white supremacy and they do its bidding better than Willie lynch, a somewhat clever theorist who sought to engineer of black disunity, could have ever imagined. The microscopic amoeba would stand no chance if one vied in a contest of smallness against a **Samboite**. It is this third group that inspired my writing but I want all three to feel the sting of my pen.

For the militant group and many in the second group, Blackness itself is the lazy explanation for every defect, dysfunction, breakdown, every smear and stain they witness in the black individuals and the black community as a whole. Blackness is their master key to explain every ponderable imperfection they imagine, from why a Black juvenile broke a window pane to why a black mechanic shop failed to fix a car or keep its commercial word. For them, it is blackness that burglarizes a house or traffics illegal drugs, not misguided individuals who just happen to be Black.

Their heads would explode like a grenade if Cheikh

21

Anta Diop's knowledge of African history landed too suddenly in his/her brain. These woefully uninformed individuals have had me looking back and wondering how much of the meanness I saw as a youth being directed toward black children by black adults was inspired by the Sambo Virus. It strikes terror in my heart to speculate how many of them are in my own extended family, let alone the Black family as a whole.

I don't pretend to know their numbers. I'm not even sure I would want to know. But if the attitudes I have personally encountered, heard about, observed up close, or seen by satellite is a representative sample, then poverty of every kind will be ours for many years to come, barring a revolution.

# CHAPTER II
## IN OUR OWN BLACK YARD

To some it may sound like something out of the twilight zone, but there *are* Black people who harbor racist views toward the black race. The idea may seem so preposterous on the surface that it is easily dismissed as either runaway imagination or a sensational claim concocted to sell a book. I plead guilty only to wanting to sell my book.

But I must enter a "not guilty" plea to prove that it is not just my imagination. Although I am no longer in denial about the reality of Samboism or Black people hating Black people, I still prefer the "good old days" when we had only to contend with white racism, or so it seemed.

This is what I made myself believe as a student at Savannah State College in Savannah Georgia when I first heard about the phenomenon. I tricked myself into believing it wasn't real.

I don't recall the specific topic of discussion that led up to what was for me an earth-shaking moment, but I clearly remember a psychology professor, during a lecture in my psychology 101 class, making a parenthetical statement in which she declared "Black people hate each other".

Upon hearing these words I looked around the classroom to see if any other faces registered the revulsion that her words aroused in my then eighteen year old brain. The proverbial ton of bricks hit me in the head.

Ironically, in a class that introduced fundamental ideas about the workings of the human psyche, I wound up going into a mode of denial and self-deception, using defense mechanisms the mind employs to cope with unpleasant experiences. After ruminating on the shocking statement for a few seconds, I dismissed the professor's words as academic overkill. But a seed of suspicion was thereby planted in the back of my mind.

Over the years that followed I came across literature that made reference to Black self-hate. This, combined with some of my own reflections and observations, led me to give some credibility to the idea, but I still didn't see it as ubiquitous or as consequential as I see it today. Surely its invisibility to me at the time had something to do with the fact that the suspects, like the ones I see today so clearly were wearing real black faces, which threw me off.

Thus, it is understandable for me that the idea of black self hate may not easy for some to digest.

I would not want to make it harder than it may already be to swallow by suggesting that your sweet aunt Essie, who is black herself, hates you the way white supremacists hate you because of your blackness. I am also not saying that all those black people who go to your church, visit your house, and laugh and talk to each other everyday, hate you and other black people this way. But, bear in mind your uncle Charlie could be a **Samboite**, some of whose anti-black sentiments functionally rival the most ardent white supremacist in intensity.

Even sweet aunt Essie can still love you yet believe or suspect you have inherent shortcomings owing to your blackness. Or, she may want you to get a haircut because that "nappy stuff" she hates, is approaching full bloom.

A main difference between Whites who hate Black people and Black people who hate Black people is the fact that the former is almost always on duty in the presence of Blacks whereas the latter is off duty most of the time in the company of his racial kinsmen. Because the Black Negrophobe's to's and fro's are so filled with blackness, he/she has to tip-toe force himself to stereotype his black brothers and sisters while his white counterpart can stand flat-footed and make it happen, whether he sees something or not.

Black hatred or dislike of Blackness is more academic and cerebral in nature than that felt by white bigots. But that we ourselves feel can be just as consequential and problematic in proportion to our power to discriminate. Of course, we have all witnessed a misguided few black individuals distance themselves from everything they consider Black, including black neighbors and even their own family members. We satisfy ourselves by dismissing them as uppity deluded freaks and cracking jokes about them behind their backs.

But even on our side of the tracks, there are those of African decent who smile and interact with us daily as "friends", spouses, mothers, fathers, neighbors, sisters and brothers, and aunts and uncles, while harboring and/or indirectly expressing beliefs about the inherent inferiority of the black race. This, by definition, makes them racist. If a white person openly expressed the slightest hint that he/she held such views about black nature, we would not hesitate for a second to brand the individual with some unwelcome title such as bigot or racist.

This is a good test to use when identifying Samboites and other Blackteria. Imagine some of the anti-black things you've heard coming from the mouths of black people coming from a person of European decent and see how it makes you feel.

We should not however, expect Samboites to burn crosses or even express a burning desire to segregate him/herself from other black people. Cross burning and separatism are not hallmarks of black Negrophobes as may be the case with white Negrophobes.

What sets the black self hater apart is the set of

beliefs they may or may not openly express, his woeful neglect of black business even when support is clearly to his/her immediate economic advantage, his/her passive acceptance of injustice toward black people, and, most telling, his/her readiness to see bad in black and good in white.

But the issue is really not whether Black self-hate is the same thing as white hatred of Black. The issue is whether or not *any* black on black hate/dislike is problematic.

However intense it is or whatever names it deserves to be called, it is baggage that weighs a people down and causes it to deprive itself and the rest of the world of the full reservoir of its genius.

The Blackteria, by spreading anti-black propaganda throughout the Black community and passing it on to future generations, destroy and undermine confidence, which is way more important than some may imagine. They do it casually, in serious conversation, small talk, and humor. They even do it from the pulpit.

We must revoke their license to do so. None of it is cute, accurate or inconsequential. How will we ever generate the momentum to work as hard as we need to work to solve our problems if the masses believe a Herculean task has to be achieved working with people who are lazy, untrustworthy, oversexed, and lacking in intelligence?

We should not be surprised, for example, when any of our young men think of our young women as little more than meat for carnal indulgence and then set it

27

to music.

Among the Blackteria, especially the Malcolm Vacuums, the belief that Africa is a jungle, inhabited by half-naked spear-chuckers, still survives at this late date in our history. There are even black college graduates who are as ignorant about Africa as they think Africans are about civilized life. Never mind that Africans were the inventors of civilization.

Even more damnable is the Samboite who uses the spiritually murderous phrase, "A Nigger ain't S--t" in the presence of young impressionable minds. I've heard it more times than I care to remember.

The user is, however, certainly on target about one of the people he slanders with the slur: the one he sees in the mirror when he's home alone. The individual who uses such phrases tends to be so devoid of general knowledge until, if he or she never spoke another word, no one would ever notice.

As alluded to in the introduction, my Samboite should not be confused with high-profile "uncle Toms", who serve as supreme court justices, California congressmen, muddleheaded preachers who denounce Jessie Jackson and Louis Farrakhan as racist, or nice, safe, or silent black faces on public boards who need black faces. Of course I despise these types too but they are not the extent of our in-house betrayal problem. Ironically, some Uncle Toms can be symbolically healthy for us by serving as visible icons of wrong-headedness, helping to protect our precious little reserves of loyalty. Cow manure stinks but it's still good fertilizer. I see the individual we like to label "Uncle Tom" as more strategic than hostile in his betrayal than the Samboite. The Samboite is roughly the opposite in this respect. Samboites accept at face value the dysfunction they see in the black community. They suffer from what I call "phenomenological blindness", which means they interpret what they see as absolute, without factoring in the social causes or the etiology of the phenomena they witness. Their powers of reason tend to be low to moderate. Of course, Samboites and Uncle Toms sometime come in the same Black body.

The Samboite "presees" or expects to see defects in Black people and their enterprises. Conversely, he/she expects and makes him/herself see good things in people of European decent. When the European sneezes, the Samboite hears a symphony.

The typical Unblack "doesn't see color", to cite one of their pet phrases. I strongly suspect these to be more words of cowardice than words of sincere, heartfelt philanthropy.

The Unblack's greatest fear is that somebody might see his/her naked personality not wearing the garments of pretense, which come in the form of college degrees, fraternity/sorority membership, fancy cars and clothes.

They dare not risk their "good" standing with the establishment by being too visible resisting injustice to black people or being too vocal against Eurocentrism in general. They tend to be faithful conformists and they hate it when you disturb their sleep.

Where did all this come from? No doubt our spiritual

and material poverty, both derived from racial injustice and oppression, have fostered deviant behavior which untutored minds see as confirmation of the stereotypes. Of course its origin can be traced to our ancestor's ground zero exposure to raw expressions of white supremacy. Many of the intellectual toxins we ingest today have been passed down from generation to generation.

In summary, the twisted minds of Black self-haters house some degree and form of contempt for blackness based on some combination of several things: the stereotypes, the osmotic incorporation of Eurocentric standards of beauty, face value interpretations of the breakdowns or dysfunction they see up close and in the news, the tribal images of Africa, and a daily dose of other sights, sounds, and signals that quietly proclaim WHITE IS RIGHT.

Then there is that nameless creature of self-hate created by self-hate. In other words, meanness inspired by self-hate tends to stack higher the reason some black people hate the black race. What a mess! But the news is not all bad. There are some spiritually healthy Black people who seem to me to be reincarnations of pre-dynastic Egyptians. I call them "Pre- Legrees" and "M-Spirits" (See, The Dictionary of Black Logic).

## CHAPTER III
## SNAKE, SNAILS, PUPPY DOG TALES

It is my firm belief that a great number of us need to be persuaded to believe something that we profess to already believe or think we already believe: that Black people, as a group, are not genetically inferior after all.

If we have people as enlightened as Nobel Prize winners are supposed to be, openly declaring their belief in Black inferiority, then what's to stop the average person, Black or White, from secretly embracing the same idea?

From a popular standpoint, the belief in genetic equality rests mostly on sentiment. I think this is extremely dangerous.

Have we, as a people, adequately addressed the

issue? Do we see the myth as consequential enough to warrant all out war against it?

I wrote this book because my answer to both questions is "no". I'm certainly not blaming Black people for not adequately addressing the problem. God knows we've had our hands and heads full with other race-based issues.

What I mean to say is that the time has come for us to persuade Black people themselves that any similarities between us and the beings of mythology is either in the jaundiced eye of the beholder or a set of predictable human responses to certain stimuli.

While I wish there was a pill we could all take to make our minds "pre-legree", I know that healing our attitudes toward blackness will not be easy by a long shot. There is no respectable Kierkegaardian Leap from self hate to self love. The self love that breaks cycles will come only with the acquisition of crystallized knowledge of who we are, which will in turn dissolve the thought patterns that inhibit the manhood we need.

Thus this chapter is not per se an argument against the ideas of white supremacy but rather a call to examine the assumptions upon which its ideology was built. The house of white supremacy as an idea is still standing, but its framework is made of imaginary brick and mortar and its foundation, Eurocentric historiography, is cracked and crumbling.

This is one of the reasons why the question of the racial identity of the ancient Egyptians and their cultural diffusion in antiquity is so important. Once the

Afrocentric theory settles in one's mind, one who still subscribes to the assumptions of white supremacy is burdened with the preposterous conclusion that inferior people developed civilization first and then spread its fruit to "superior" primitives.

IQ scores, another spade of white supremacy's trump cards, will never satisfy us dissenters who reject their validity, until a test is devised which discounts any experiential advantage. Despite claims to the contrary, there is no such thing as a culture-fair IQ test. It is impossible to create one. For me the best argument against the comparative racial scores is the fact that the gap tends to shrink (in some cases favor black testees) when results are adjusted for certain socioeconomic factors. It logically follows that no two humans, not even monozygotic twins, have the same experiences by the time they sit down to take an IQ test. Comparative cognitive abilities will only, if ever, be accurately measured by a machine or by observing human performance for a whole lifetime on a perfectly even playing field.

I said all this to say that as an Afrocentric apologist, I am not afraid of an objective examination of either the theoretical assumptions of IQ testing or world history. When I was growing up as a young boy, I stood up to a feared bully and thereby discovered that he was more bark than bite.

## CHAPTER IV
## THE HIGH TECH EFFECT

It is not at all unreasonable to suppose that a great number of our brothers and sisters either consciously or subconsciously believe in the intellectual superiority of Europeans as a group. One of the main reasons for this belief stems from what I call the "High Tech Effect", wherein Black people attribute superior brainpower to whites on the basis of "their" technological and/or literary achievements. It is not as easy as it appears for Black Americans to truly believe in the genetic equality of the races when our minds are bombarded throughout our casual and formal educational experiences with "IQ Icons" such as Einstein, Shakespeare, and Thomas Edison.

Such men have been virtually deified in textbooks, lore and Hollywood while our savants hardly receive honorable mention.

Black history month alone is not nearly enough to bring about our comparative self respect as Dr. Carter G. Woodson, the pioneer of Black History Month, no doubt envisioned.

The "High Tech Effect" scares me to death as I suspect even some of our best Afrocentrists are haunted by its illusions. By calling the "High Tech Effect" an illusion, I do not mean to imply that white individuals do not make meaningful contributions to civilization, but somehow their accomplishments have been wrongly inflated in some of our minds. It is as if white people have a monopoly on intelligence.

It could be argued that this is an unintended consequence of being in the numerical minority in America. Native Americans could and probably do register similar complaints. This lets nobody off the hook because much of what is written unnecessarily distorts and disfigures historical truth to favor white supremacy. (It is our job to go and get the truth) The intellectual contributions of Black people to American society in the last two hundred years, even without considering the deleterious effects of psychological oppression, would, by itself, be very impressive. But, when one factors them in, our achievements become mind boggling.

Even on the very uneven playing field, a seemingly disproportionate number of superlatives precede and follow Black names such as the "first successful open heart surgery, the "world's greatest living scientist" (called Carver by Henry Ford), the first traffic light, the world's greatest living poet (called Smokey Robinson by several people in the pop world). One of the names is even an eponym for something that is considered authentic, the "real McCoy", named for a Black inventor Elijah McCoy.

When we consider the low percentage of Black people in America, Black pioneering and quintessence defy statistical probability. Simply put, in a strict statistical sense, our numbers are not great enough in America to produce what we have produced.

Yes, it is true that we are over represented in crime and other indices of social deviance, but we are over represented in some good stuff too.

But while we could enumerate inventions, scientific breakthroughs, and discoveries by African Americans all day long, they will not deliver the knock out punch I'd love to deliver to the "High Tech Effect" and the Pigment Figment altogether.

This is where our remote past comes in. To begin with, there is simply no way an inferior subspecies or stock of human beings could have done what our ancestors did.

As it turns out, much of what we call western civilization is intellectually rooted in African thought. So many fundaments, whose creative seeds and fruit nourish our moral and technological lives today, sprung from Black minds. Were it not for the diffusion of mathematics, geometry, and other sciences from Africa to the rest of the world, our much-vaunted rocket science for example, would still be science fiction if anything at all. (by now it should be clear that

I have very little respect for arguments against the Afrocentric "theory" of Ancient Egypt. Quite frankly, I find some of them laughable and others neurotic).

Even if a Eurocentrist accepted the Afrocentric theory, he would probably still argue that today's technological know-how and insights are vastly superior to that of the ancients.

First of all, it *should* be superior if it is not, since we have the old and the new to build on. The foundational knowledge Egypt and Nubia passed on to the moderns is very much a part, maybe even the most important part, of the progress the world has made. The son of Frankenstein should be expected to build a better monster than his father because he, unlike his father, didn't have to start from scratch.

Einstein didn't build an atomic bomb but his theory led the understanding of the tremendous potential energy stored in matter. Yet almost no one would say Robert Oppenheimer, who headed up the famous Manhattan Project, by which this Godforsaken weapon was constructed, was a greater scientist than Einstein.

Besides all this, the building of the pyramids alone bespeaks powers of the mind that at least arguably have not been rivaled since.

Those who are awe-stricken by modern technology should ask themselves where Africa would be technologically if ancient Egypt had never been invaded by cultural neophytes from the outside.

I used to tell my son and daughter that we might've been having dinner at nice restaurant on Jupiter or some other planet in our solar system instead of getting take out from Church's Fried Chicken here on earth.

## CHAPTER V
## EVERY DAY IS 911

Black America can learn something from the Bush administration's response the events of September 11, 2001. I will leave to the pundits to argue whether or not it acted in good faith launching a military campaign in Iraq, but ostensibly, it did what we in the Black community have every reason to do: go on offense and defense seeking to nullify immediate and long-range threats to the security and welfare of our people. Bush and company did not sit around and wait on the United Nations or anybody else, just as Black Americans should not sit around and wait on any division or subdivision of government to protect us and our children from the threats that can be neutralized with a change of consciousness. What ever we do we should do with a sense of urgency. It is truly a matter of life and death.

Gang violence, for example, is a threat to black Americans whether we are in a gang ourselves or not. (Gang violence is one of the children of poverty and dysfunction. Poverty and dysfunction are in turn the grandchildren of racial oppression.)

Our lives and the quality of our lives are threatened and taken everyday by poverty, famine, disease, academic failure, police brutality, unnecessary incarceration, moral decay, heart disease, and a long list of other disorders. Our spiritual health, whose recovery would go a long way toward alleviating if not eliminating these breakdowns, suffers at the hand of Eurocentrism and the psychological legacy of self hate.

More people die of hunger and disease on any given day than the number who perished on 911 and a high percentage of them are Black. We should've long had the same sense of urgency that that day created in Americans in general.

All of this means that we can ill-afford neutral, "zerocentric" mindsets that you are likely to find among Unblacks and Malcolm Vacuums.

I know very well that most Black Americans do not possess an anti-white mentality and that is not what I am advocating. I am advocating rather a problack mentality because regardless of who is to blame, we have a mess with which to contend and it requires us to focus on race-based concerns to get ourselves out of it.

We must address the root causes of the problems and their very visible by products with new approaches.

The American consciousness was changed by the events of 911 and ours could be changed just as abruptly if we inventoried all that is wrong and threatening to us.

What happened to those innocent people and their surviving family members was a great tragedy to say the least. But what is happening to Black people in America and the world over is also tragic and probably more preventable. We may not see it like that because the death-dealing circumstances tend to be temporally scattered and not as spectacular as what happened in New York on that infamous day. We should be terrified. None of us are immune. No matter who we are in Black America, we are all equally responsible for turning things around. The fact that we are victims of white supremacy makes us no less responsible for other Black victims than anyone else. We must stop waiting to advance on the bloodshed of the few and progress on the sweat of the many.

## CHAPTER VI
## MAMA TRAUMA

The greater part of the thing we call personality is derived from how a child sees himself being seen by the world. In the case of most African-American children, the mother is the primary shaper of the image he sees being seen. Of course other people and impressions help form the final one that emerges. It is only human to prefer seeing ourselves being seen as positive in every way in the eyes of all in our immediate circles and the rest of the world. If, for example, a child sees the world seeing his skin as too dark, his lips too thick, his hair too kinky , as is often the case of many Black children , he is apt to build a set of personality traits around the anxieties produced by these "deficits". If his mother, immediate environment, and the world at large send him direct and subtle signals that being of African descent and all that it implies, is undesirable, he may be forever filled with doubts about himself and suspicious of virtually all those who share his genetic heritage. He may see himself as a bad apple in a barrel of bad apples. This is not the developmental recipe for well-adjusted individuals. It is certainly not the formula for creating paragons of virtue, champions of justice, or captains of industry. It is a miracle that we are more than reasonably represented in these three areas of leadership.

Unfortunately, what many African American children see and have seen being seen by mom and the rest of the world has been contaminated by the "Sambo Virus" and the "Pigment Figment"

The negative ideas about Blackness often conspire with high levels of socioeconomic stress and render Black children vulnerable to displaced anger and frustration. Their parents, some of whom are Samboites and Malcolm Vacuums, may sometimes relate to them, especially children with pronounced Negroid features, in harsh vituperative language, which sometimes extend to the child's hair texture and skin complexion. This tends to produce self-doubting, affection-starved children and adolescents who compensate in anti-social and often dangerous ways.

If we are to cure ourselves of the Sambo Virus and its effects, we will have to develop a special consciousness aiming to nourish and protect our children during what I call the "Ought to Eight" (0 to 8

43

years old). Black mothers and others must recognize motherhood as a major battleground on which to resist the effects of racial injustice, its psychological legacy, and its present-day manifestations.

Potential parents must loudly and proudly favor conjugal procreation and pledge to give their children the super important advantage of a good mom and a good dad. Actual parents must hug, kiss and praise them, especially during the **ought to eight** period, while, at the same time, fighting any inhibition or frustration which might make them act otherwise.

Secular leaders must protect their psychological development from both interracial and intra-racial expressions of anti-blackness.

Religious leaders must work from the pulpit to enshrine family values, especially as they pertain to fatherhood.

And, neighbors must honor the African proverb which charges the village with raising the child.

It is all very simple. Either we find more space for our children in our hearts or more space will be built for them by the penal system.

## CHAPTER VII
## ROMANTIC LOVE AND SELF HATE

"I will build you a castle with a tower so high, it reaches the moon; I'll gather melodies from birdies that fly, and compose you a tune," begins the Miracles 1960's hit song "I'll Try Something New".

Three decades later the lyrics "All I wanna do is zoom my zoom zoom zoom at a boom boom", could be heard in a popular rap song being played on radio stations all over America. Most of those old enough to have lived in both eras would probably agree in a heartbeat that the second song comes closer to representing the present-day attitude of our young Black men toward our young black women.

Let me say before proceeding that I am not blaming today's music for the problems of Black America because I believe it is more of a barometer than it is bad weather. But at the same time I also believe popular music can and sometimes does, accelerate moral decay.

But whatever the sources of our problems, remedial approaches can become effective only when we spotlight and focus on the critical points of breakdowns. I happen to believe that one of the most pivotal points of our struggle is that of Romantic love. Not only is this pillar breaking down, it is speeding fast toward the debauchery we associate with the biblical Sodom and Gomorrah. No doubt, our general disrespect for the Black collective, figures heavily in its decline. Too much of what is wrong and repairable in Black America hinges on the opposite sex's view of each other's romantic worthiness for us to take it as lightly as we do.

Not only should we be concerned about the loose, vulturous attitudes toward sexuality in our young men but it should also terrify us that ours, the subculture, and the greater culture, seems to have fallen out of love with romance. Where are the Smokey Robinsons, the Curtis Mayfields and other pop poets whose lyrics and beautiful ballads helped guard our reverence and respect for Black women and romance in general? We could certainly use a rapid return to the mindsets of their bygone eras.

This is not important to me just because I am sentimental or even because the thought of so many lovelorn black women who deserve better breaks my own heart. I am also concerned with the trickle down effects of a healthy man-woman culture to our children and their emotional development.

A child is far more likely to receive emotional nourishment from his parents if the two are married and in love.

The African proverb that says "The hand that rocks the cradle is the hand that rules the world" is for me a golden truth that should've been included in the New Testament. It was divinely inspired to help keep our attitudes toward our women in check because women are the most important shapers of these emotionally fragile little human beings.

But if the "hand that rock the cradle" is, itself, constantly rocked by rocky relationships, the chances for her properly doing her part are greatly diminished.

Yet there is a trail of broken hearts of Black women who still have old-fashioned expectations at a time when monogamy seems more like an urban legend than the Christian ideal where young men are concerned.

Today we witness the enshrinement of promiscuity as signified most aptly by young men fashionably referring to each other as "playa".

I am not saying that Black women are perfect because a few of them are not. But it is the man who misbehaves on the playground of romance.

They are the products of a negatively charged atmosphere that will continue to shock us unless we make major changes in how we do business.

Ideally, a man should feel something wide and deep for the woman who would bear his children, before

47

she conceives.

To that end we must somehow put to death the desire of our young men to paint themselves with frigid, Laodicean romantic personas toward young women who attract them physically. Our women should be rewarded with monogamous men and be showered with affection and affectionate words that don't address their backsides.

If we can manage to get our thoughts past their naturally beautiful faces and figures, we would see a delicate, unsung femininity that I believe is culturally unrivaled.

When we men realize what we have in black women, there might be groundbreaking ceremonies in Black America every day for a new Taj Mahal.

We must end the silence from the pulpits on the messiness of our boy-girl relationship trends and tendencies. We must make a joyful noise about the subject of romance in the streets, in the barbershops, behind podiums or in front of TV cameras. Our young men and some old men should learn that there is platonic pleasure too to be derived from the company of our beautiful maidens.

They must know that there is much more to the opposite sex than just sex.

We must put a new generation of song poets in recording studios churning out songs like "The Makings of You" and "My Girl". And "if that don't do", then *we* should try something new.

## CHAPTER VIII
## WE'RE NOT IN ANCIENT AFRICA ANYMORE, TODO

Some of the following true stories affected my sleep on the day or the night following the day of their occurrence or the day they were told to me. My own personal encounters with white-on-black racism never bothered me as much since virtually none of them were utter surprises.

If pressed I could probably produce a hundred or more such accounts as
could any clear thinking Black American tuned in to what is happening around him or her.

They are stories of my personal encounters with Blackteria and anecdotes shared with me by kindred spirits.

What these stories have in common is that each of them signifies that we need to wage war against the anti-black thought patterns they bespeak.

Imagine that the unnamed characters were white, although all of them were in reality of African decent. Imagine how you would feel if your were there witnessing the imaginary whites saying exactly what black people themselves were saying about the black race.

**The dollar store**

As my wife and I waited at the front of a check out line of a dollar store in Macon Georgia we overheard a light-hearted exchange between two young African American cashiers. The first cashier said to the other "you wanna know why you didn't pay me my gas money"? The second cashier obliged with the expected "why". The first cashier replied "because you black".

Had my wife and I been white, they probably would not have spoken as freely as they did. But it was obvious to me and my wife that they didn't mind us overhearing what they said to each other. That, in and of itself, bothered me because it suggested that they had "good" reason to believe that all Black people already know about such self-evident defects in our kind.

This particular "defect" in Black people had something to do with not honoring debt. I will not argue that these young ladies had not seen a certain frequency of delinquency on a small or large scale.

But I doubt seriously if either of them had the faintest idea how often white people default on small financial obligations like helping to pay for gas when one catches a ride with the other.

I have to believe that this was no more than a sweeping generalization whose invocation came from no where except that counterfeit region of their sick brains where misconception and preconceptions about black people are stored.

These two women are likely to continue spreading contaminated ideas in their social circles. Maybe I should have said something to the young ladies which might have inspired them to think about what they were saying. But I did nothing except stand there and bite my tongue.

There was a fleeting thought in my mind about asking to speak to the manager and registering a complaint about being exposed to racially offensive dialogue by store employees.

It is not a stretch to imagine that most black people would have done what I was tempted to do had the two cashiers been white speaking of black people in the third person. The race of the criminals in this case makes no difference.

Yet I unwisely and perhaps selfishly chose silence. I wanted to preserve my "dignity" and not risk being thought of as a kooky black man, upset by an "innocuous", rather commonplace exchange. I have since asked myself who was, in this case, less loyal to the black cause between the three of us. I finally decided that my selfish silence was worse than what they said. Their ignorant words were more innocent than my silence. In the highest moral sense I should consider myself partly responsible for whatever spiritual damage they might do to black minds in the future saying such things without compunction.

I have been challenged many times by my wife and daughter after they witness me challenging a black person for saying something anti-black or racist toward black people.

These are the two most important women in my life and they never take issue with *why* I respond, but only *how* I respond.

It sometimes makes them uncomfortable especially when my adversary is someone close to us by association or by blood. They believe my passion sometimes makes me sound threatening although I never use profanity or say things to berate the sinner deliberately.

I sometimes feel like Johnny Cochran trying to persuade O.J. Simpson that he didn't kill his ex wife and Ronald Goldman.

Whereas I consider both my wife and daughter to be very able thinkers, I often accuse them of looking for the path of least resistance when they chastise me in this respect. They nevertheless advocate more tact on my part. It is my guess that almost everybody would favor their approach over a more confrontational one. But I am not so sure. I do not have a standard approach for challenging expressions of self-hate/disrespect in Black people.

The only thing I am sure about is that silence wrong

every time.

Socrates submitted a series of questions designed to expose falsehood.

Jesus turned over a table and called the Pharisees hypocrites, snakes and vipers.

Non-confrontational finesse probably has its place when it comes to trying to change minds. But I sometimes fantasize being able to morph into a werewolf like Lon Chaney, Jr. used to do in those old black and white horror movies every time I was in the presence of a black person who said something to cast black people in a negative light. That way I might frighten people away from spreading their poisonous ideas to young impressionable minds.

Maybe in the future a Black social scientist will study and devise the best approach to responding to Samboite statements, but in the meantime, apologists like me should not be handcuffed with too many doubts about their approaches.

Once again, silence is the worst approach and there is too much at stake.

Generations of unborn black babies are crying for us to do the right thing right now.

## The barber shop encounter

A young Afrocentric apologist told me that while he waited to get a haircut one day another man who was also waiting was "bragging" that he had Indian blood.

This apologist, as should be expected, finds it irksome when African Americans say things that suggest that they are ashamed of their African heritage.

To be fair, the braggart may very well have been sharing this information as a matter of fact and not, as the apologist suspected, to throw off shame of his blackness. But the apologist didn't see it that way and I would bet the mortgage that the apologist was right.

In a tone of suppressed but detectable contempt, the apologist asked the braggart if he attached any self esteem to his Indian heritage. The braggart of course denied this and also denied the implication that he was running from his Blackness.

I find it highly improbable that the braggart embraced his Indian genes on the basis of his knowledge of the admirable ancient Mayans, Incas, or the Aztecs. (Who evidently had cultural ties to ancient Africa).

Like many Americans his perception of Native Americans was probably derived from the unrepresentative lore extracted from Hollywood depiction and street talk.

This leaves nothing but his desire to dilute his unwelcome African physicality and make sure others know he is not all black.

In the apologist's defense, I am certain that he was not at all attempting to demean Native Americans in any way, but rather, trying to sting this lost soul's bland thought process into a beehive busy with questions and a different set of reflections.

**My college roommate**

Savannah State College had been functioning for decades before I or my roommate enrolled in this wonderful institution. As far as I know, its registrar's office had always been staffed by Black Americans, at least predominately, if not 100 percent. I can only say for sure that everyone I ever saw working there was of African decent. Yet in a casual discussion, my roommate, upon hearing two other students talking about a matriculation error the school apparently made at one or both of their expense, stated boldly, "they need a white man in that office".

I had been in this school of higher learning long enough to know that there was no epidemic outcry about such errors. In my personal case, there was never the slightest miscue in four years.

My roommate was seeing black behavior through a prism of mythology which primed his mind to see even racially proportionate deviance or human error as disproportionate and confirm his mastery of a counterfeit body of knowledge.

Many Black Americans have no idea whatsoever that their minds are filled with toxic levels of anti-black fictions which directly and indirectly affect the quality of their lives. Many of their strings of perception are being pulled by long-dead puppeteers.

**The Hotel**

My wife and I were approaching the lobby of a hotel when we were approached by a Black female hotel employee en route to the same destination.

"Can I help you", she asked, in a tone of voice somewhere between robotic and contemptuous. Either way she didn't greet us with any measure of warmth nor did she smile. We responded by saying "We want to get a room, please". Her very next words, in pretty much the same tone as her first set, were, "What kind of room", inflecting her voice as if every time people ask to rent a room they always specify first the "kind" of room they want. We walked away after telling her in a relatively similar tone of voice that we changed our mind because of her attitude. She then walked away as if nothing out of the ordinary had happened.

My wife was livid. I was at first more puzzled than upset. We talked about submitting a formal complaint but decided against it since we didn't want the woman to lose her job. Since I am not omniscient I can only guess her attitude was inspired by the Sambo Virus.

**A Teacher Confesses**

A young African American elementary school teacher broke my heart when she said flatly that white children were smarter than black children. What she was judging was academic performances, which very often, especially in the case of African American students, belie God-given intelligence.

I hope this teacher never finds out if she hasn't already, about the gap in IQ test scores because surely that will confirm for her a fallacious point of view.

How in Heaven's name will anybody ever persuade

her that these "scientifically" designed instruments don't tell the truth when what she sees every day in the classrooms "proves" it? Dear reader, this is what we are up against.

## Miseducation

Another college mis-educated Black person was shocked to learn that they have schools in Africa. Perhaps he would have had a stroke if he was shown indisputable proof that the first schools in the world started on the mother continent.

Another college graduate was shocked to learn that they have money in Africa. So many of our people have so much to "unlearn".

A young man on my staff once asked rhetorically "What difference does it make whether Egypt is in Africa".

If the dictum, "Man, Know Thyself" points us to the highest level of knowledge, then people who have to ask such questions are but spiritual kindergarteners.

To know that Egypt is in Africa is to give at least slightly more credibility to the Afrocentric theory of Egypt which is but a faint rumor in many black minds but gospel truth to some. To believe that Ancient Egypt was a Black civilization clips the wings of the idea of an inherently barbaric black race of Africa. To know that Egypt was the key player in civilizing the world, potentially puts the whole idea of Black inferiority to rest.

## A sick doctor

A very spiritually sick Samboite openly compared favorably the behavior of white boys he had worked with earlier to what he considered unruly behavior of the large group of adolescent African-American boys he addressed. I'm just glad my son, who was in the same age range at the time, was not in his audience, for my son's sake and because I might have lost my cool in response to the whole thing.

No matter what other credentials or attributes one might possess, a person with this type spirit and ignorance should not be allowed to speak in such a setting.

A few days later another speaker in the same setting spoke to the boys with an unnecessarily harsh tone attempting to quiet them down. Shortly after they did get quiet, he told them that Black male slaves "allowed" white men to rape and abuse their daughters and wives and did nothing to stop it.

This time I was present, and was hit with a sense of urgency to neutralize this misinformation. I explained to the boys that the men slaves knew well that it would be suicide to act in a manner the clueless speaker implied was more appropriate. I also explained to them that some of the slaves did indeed give up their lives trying to protect their families.

Of all the eight or nine baby-boomers who spoke to these impressionable young minds that day, I personally would have felt comfortable with only two of the bunch addressing a group that included my son.

**The mis-educated basketball coach**

Somehow amidst a smörgåsbord of two way conversations, group discussions, and loud laughter, a playful dispute between two girl high school basketball players, both named Dorothy, and both bearing the nick-name "Dot", captured the spotlight. Almost everybody on the school bus that night tuned in to their exchange, including the young male basketball coach who was sitting next to me.

We were on our way home from out of town games from which our girls and boys emerged with a victory. Both teams were highly competitive.

The young basketball coach had a fresh college education and, looking back, a not-so-fresh mis-education.

I hope the coach has learned better by now, but evidently, at least at the time, he, like many of his peers, believed White people were some kind of intellectual super race.

When somebody on the bus that night submitted a robust request for the two girls to settle their benign quarrel, I responded out loud, deliberately trying to be funny, "you put two dots together, they won't end anything but a sentence".

The young coach, who was sitting in front of me, turned around, looked at me, squinted and said "David Hunter, you are very intelligent (he stressed, very) intelligent for a young Black man. The compliment felt good at the time, but I also recall it fading to bittersweet when I realized he was also

59

saying that I was a part of a genetically defective group of people when compared to Whites.

I wasn't all that shocked that this young teacher/coach thought the way he did, but I was somewhat puzzled and a bit frustrated as to what made people really believe such things.

I knew about slavery but I also knew at the time that the supposedly White Greeks were held in bondage by the white Romans. I didn't at the time know about the gap in IQ test scores (which is a joke, by the way and another book I may try to write) but neither did most of the people in my social circle. Even today it is not widely known. I honestly don't remember ever believing any of the myths about the superiority of people of European decent.

But evidently the young coach fancied himself on par with white people, maybe even superior to the average one. I know no other way to explain the fact that he was smiling while complementing me at the expense of the race to which he himself belongs.

**Ye old African**

My nephew was peeved at something my half brother, who shared living quarters with him at the time, had said or done. I don't remember the beginning of my nephew's complaint, but I do recall him disparagingly saying that his uncle, my half brother, was "acting like an old African". Although I had heard many such remarks as a young boy growing up, this one was stunning to me only a few years from the turn of the new century.

It made me realize that I had not accurately televised my beliefs else my nephew would not have said what he said so freely in my presence. I believe he loves and respects me.

Evidently simple worldviews saw me as more anti-white than pro-black.

.    It also made me realize that my nephew, like many of our brothers and sisters, simply didn't know any better. Where would he and other Malcolm Vacuums have learned better? I love him still. I freely admit that all the people that inspired this book can plea and make this their defense.

But however mitigating ignorance may be, it does not change the fact that they need to and may, in some cases, submit to an intellectual ass-whipping from me. (Even at the risk of being on the receiving end of a physical one myself).

I finally told my nephew that he had just paid his uncle a high compliment calling him an African. He caught my drift but probably didn't take me seriously about the high compliment claim. I also remember taking a page from one of my best friend's unwritten, but brilliant book of logic, reminding my nephew that he too was African, and so were his father, mother, grandmother, grandfather, and all his kin. So what does that say about them? I also informed him that if, by African, he meant a being of subhuman intelligence, undesirable physical bearings, stuck in a state of barbarism until the handsome, superior European rescues him, he had just demeaned and dehumanized me, himself, his uncle and all those from which we sprang.

As I sat there stewing on my nephew's "criticism" of his "African" uncle, I somehow managed to contain myself (I sometimes fail, miserably). In another setting at another time, I might have, and probably should have told him that all continents, including Africa, have tribal groups and his mind is just Tarzan- Poisoned. I might have also reminded him of the "rumors" he no doubt had heard, that civilization began in Africa and that what we call tribalism today is relatively new to the motherland, and that black people once looked down on white people the way he apparently looks down on Black people today.

Perhaps foolishly, I held my peace when I should have given my nephew a piece of my mind. But to his credit, he didn't argue or mindlessly defend himself at that little tonal spanking I gave him.

# CHAPTER IX
## ABSTRACT BLACK

My insatiable appetite for hearing and seeing expressions of Black self-love makes it somewhat difficult to write or say anything negative about any Black person who openly identifies with his or her African heritage for whatever reason.

Unfortunately, the outward expression of some of these individuals does not accurately reflect the contents of their spirits. In other words, one can have an Afrocentric mind without having an Afrocentric heart.

Afrocentricity in this case becomes little more than an expression of foolish pride in many eyes.

No version of pro-blackness is as prized today in

Black America as it was in the sixties, but that which is visibly tempered by anything other than genuine love and respect for Black people stands little or no chance of being received with open arms. In fact, the opposite effect may be more likely since being too symbolically Black frightens off some Black people because they know it sometimes makes White people uncomfortable.

Afrocentricity is the most legitimate springboard to our spiritual rebirth. It is therefore nothing with which to play. Our spiritual rebirth, which is little more than the absence of the Sambo Virus, is a prerequisite to our ability to fight what ails us from both sides of the tracks.

Contrary to what many apparently believe, the recovery of our self respect and racial confidence cannot be willed into existence by any individual or any group. They must be brought about by reason and revelation, unless we discover another way to detoxify this generation and immunize the next ones from the anti-black toxins we unknowingly imbibe in America.

Strictly cosmetic or symbolic afrocentricity hurts our cause in another way. It sometimes artificially satisfies the primal desire to become whole and make others around us feel whole. It narrows the focus of its practitioners to superficiality and empty symbolism while distracting them from the need to radiate with warmth and do other things such as showing glowing signs of approval in the presence of his kinsmen, especially young children.

If I didn't know this before, I learned it one day while in a conversation with two Black Muslims and one of my best friends, Mr. J. I had run into all three men by accident while leaving the record store of a small plaza in Albany, Georgia. One of the two Muslims I had met and become friendly with earlier.

I started out talking with him before my friend spotted me and drove up in a van. Sam, the first Muslim, was Afrocentric enough, as one might expect, being a member of the Nation of Islam, but it was the second Muslim who impressed me and my friend. He did so without uttering a single Afrocentric word or phrase or using any black power sign.

It was the sheer warmth of his attitude and attitude alone that made a lasting impression on us and kept us talking about it for years to come.

The young man smiled, greeted us warmly, and bowed to us after being introduced by Sam. He smiled throughout the conversation while listening politely as the rest of us opined. His own commentary was submitted with great humility and he graciously complimented each of us for points or statements we contributed individually.

He ultimately took advantage of a momentary pause in the dialogue to excuse himself from the unplanned gathering. In doing so, he smile and bowed again.

I have seen him only once since then but his comportment that day wrote a chapter in my brain and embellished the definition of Afrocentrism in my heart.

Socrates once said that the unexamined life is not worth living. Both Mr. J and the humble young man's glowing humility inspired me to reexamine myself because I want Black people to see in me the beauty I've seen in them, not because of my ego, but because I want to be a mirror in which they can see themselves in a positive light and know how worthy they are of supreme respect, regardless of station. To me this is Afrocentricity at its best.

## CHAPTER X
### CHRISTIANITY, FRIEND OR FOE

A number of thinking black people I know have expressed to me an opinion that Christianity inhibits Black unity and hinders our cause in other ways. While this roughly captures my own beliefs, I believe they, as do I, would find it more accurate to say the absence of *true* Christianity is the essential problem.

My brother-in-law summed up my beliefs when he said, "I'm afraid we are practicing a form of Christianity that can destroy a nation".

In the course of the conversation that produced this insightful point, I told him that some historians blame Christianity for the fall of the Roman Empire.

It is most tragic that the precious teachings of Christ and his emphasis on selflessness and love are beginning to be thought of as something different from the purpose of the church.

Church membership in many instances has become a license to wink at wrong, be self-centered, and indifferent to the big pain and small pain of our brothers and sisters.

The superficial practice of Christianity hurts the black struggle in a number of ways: It often smuggles stilts of righteousness to moral midgets who stand in high places and broadcast fraudulent interpretations of holy tenants for cowardly and selfish reasons; It impersonates philanthropy and altruism and causes us to overlook the incredible shortage of these most precious commodities; It shaves the manes of lions causing us to fatally confuse them with lambs; It launders evil so we countenance it with little or no compunction; It slanders men and women who stand up so that men of lesser spirit can bow down, feel safe, and still be able to look at themselves in the mirror.

The pulpit is a magnet for individuals with low self-esteem, guilty conscious, and other by-products interpersonal chaos.

True Christianity is true love. True Christianity is bold, courageous and selfless. The church seems to address everything but these things.

Too many churchgoers attach too much importance to what goes on inside the four walls of the church while virtually ignoring the moral cesspool on the outside except for its value as gossip. We need what Jesus taught, not ecclesiolatry which we have in so many cases.

Even some people inside the church have admitted to me they are bored with a high percentage of the sermons they hear. They didn't really have to, because I have seen many asleep while lollipop lectures and popcorn points were being made by preachers whose simple words edified no one and died in the brain of the few listeners after only a few seconds of life therein.

Those of us who genuinely care about what is happening to Black people must not sit in silence while Pharisaism and vanity usurp the space and time cosmically scheduled for a genuine Christian movement against moral decay and other things that work against our recovery. We must speak out against hypocrisy as boldly as Jesus did in ancient Israel. The church must become a legitimate source of moral leadership or it will, as suggested by Bishop Shelby Spong, die of irrelevance.

To me it is most un-Christian to sit and listen at preachers who make sense only to people who have no sense.

Nobody should ever walk away from a church sermon feeling less responsible for the heartache of his brothers and sisters. Every sermon should aim to make us better emotional parents, better village parents, or better lovers of the common good, to cite a few examples.

Preachers need not be experts in parenting or any other particular field of study, but merely gatekeepers and guardians and imparters of values, creating a hunger and thirst in people to love, express love, romantic and agape.

In our quest to recover from the psychological effects of oppression, Christianity should have been our greatest ally. Instead, its hollow form has made it one of our greatest obstacles.

Church sermons have disintegrated into a theater of worthless points, with preachers serving as pied pipers who lead the flock to a sea wherein moral responsibility is drowned or passed on to divine intervention.

I am not dismissing divine intervention as a reality, but I am rather complaining that the idea is being marketed to the masses of churchgoers as a readily harness-able, over-the-counter, push-button source of power.

This fits too well with the natural inertia of human beings. This same inertia has tempted me to omit this chapter. But to do so would be to indulge in the same cowardice and blind conformity I lament.

If it is true, as some evidently believe, that God sees to it that a utility bill is paid for one person, while allowing an innocent child to perish for want of food, it follows that the divine will is far too complex for preachers to grasp intellectually, let alone mislead their congregations to believe its fruit is there for the picking.

Christianity should be, but it is not popularly emphasized as a way of life or, more specifically, as how man should relate to man. Its hollow form, which is the true darling of our affections, consumes too much of our thought process and drains us of manhood.

## CHAPTER XI
**THERE MUST BE 50 WAYS TO SAY THE N WORD**

There are several prominent Black leaders who seem concerned about the problems of Black people in general, but I can think of only a few who seem to see black self-hate/self-disrespect as something that merits major concern. I hope the reality is different from what I see. It would be ironic that the point where white supremacy has done its greatest damage, it is least resisted by the most visible black leaders. I do not mean to criticize them because in all fairness they have their hands full as it is. I just happen to believe that they should sacrifice if necessary some of their projects to address such problems. As for me, I get upset when Black comedians make fun of Africa. It bothers me even more when their audiences laugh freely when they do. It annoys me to see ancient Egyptians portrayed as anything other than black people, be it a movie, a TV documentary, or any other program.

One of the most popular science fiction films ever made, after showing a series of scenes depicting military personnel in control rooms in several different countries celebrating the defeat of the aliens, found it necessary for some reason to show tribal African warriors as part of the segment. Whether the creators of the blockbuster planned it or not, several people, no doubt, either concluded from what they saw or kept riding on the false belief, that Africa has no modern military to speak of.

Since it has been estimated that as much as 50 percent of all box office tickets in America are sold to Black people, it is more than reasonable to suppose that the false perception of Africa, its people, diasporic or continental, was reinforced.

We get mad when actors, talk show hosts, etc. use the N word maliciously, but to me, depictions like this imply something much worse. They suggest that African people are still in the Stone Age and that is where African Americans would be too were it not for the slave trade. Surely, a similar thought ran through the minds of some of the viewers. Somebody got away with calling us the N word as has happened so many times in Hollywood. You don't have to say "N---- R", to call somebody a "N----r". There must be 50 ways to do so.

I love Jessie Jackson and I love Al Sharpton. I just

wish they and others like them would use the special endowments (Both are brilliant and super articulate) to help rescue our children's delicate psyches from such cinematic toxins. We at the grassroots level must immunize our children as best we can if we can't stop the capitalistic juggernaut from saying what it wants to say without regard to truth.

In another case, a popular magazine ran a series of articles at the turn of the millennium that spotlighted supposedly "the 100 greatest minds of the twentieth century".

While I admire some of the achievements of the people featured, I do not believe for one second that this group possessed the 100 greatest minds in the last 100 years. You might argue that they were the most productive minds during that span of time, but it is highly improbable that most of the 100 most intellectually endowed people on earth came from a group that constitutes roughly 10 percent of the world's population. (Unless one believes Whites are special). It is far more probable that the best minds of the 20th century never even learned to read and write, let alone win a Nobel Prize. How is this possible? Some may have died before their first birthday from hunger or some hunger-related disease.

And then there's the ugly business of IQ testing which I personally dismiss as theoretically fraudulent. I suspect that this pseudo-scientific gap in IQ scores is quietly tucked away in the back of many White minds like a forbidden fruit, but still guarding for them, their illusory intellectual superiority.

Their performances on these test square too well with the prevailing **Pigment Figment.** Every time there is talk about IQ testing, all Black ears in listening range should know the best arguments against the its validity. When there is no response by those in the know, the users thereof have gotten away with calling us the n- word without using the n-word.

Last but not least, I can't even begin to count the number of times I have looked up and seen magazine covers with headlines to the effect "The 50 or 100 most beautiful people in the world". Guess who makes up the majority.

But for this I can only argue by saying that if a chimpanzee had written such an article titled the 50 most beautiful primates in the world, they would have, out of political correctness, thrown in sprinkling of Homo sapiens to pacify us humans. No doubt, King Kong, Mighty Joe Young, and Cheetah would be in the top ten.

## CHAPTER XII
## ONE NATION, MANY NOTIONS

It seems to be well understood in our community that Black people need to "come together". However, I am inclined to believe that more people are in love with the word "unity" than they are with unity as an existential reality. It is not that I believe they are against Black unity, but the word seems to float in a meaningless nebulous of nothingness in that part of the brain where you would find the likes of "I love everybody", or "nobody's perfect".

Yet we speak of Black unity as though it is a clearly understood or self-explanatory concept. It is a proud lion, roaring with no teeth.

It would seem that Black "unity" has eluded us in both definition and practice. The problem with the toothless definition ("coming together") is that it enables our Unblacks and others to sound pro-black situationally while being lukewarm at best toward the Black struggle. *Unity* is a face-saving buzzword that they imagine silences any potential questions about their fashionable "loyalty" to Blackness.

Ask the next person you hear saying something like "we need to come together" to elaborate further on what it means to "come together" and you may see him/her self-destruct or at least sweat to give you an answer that makes any sense at all.

I once asked a somewhat Afrocentric friend to describe for me, a unified Black America. He wound up taking umbrage to what turned out to be a challenge for him after realizing that he had been flirting with a word or words whose meaning and implications had not begun to take shape in his very good mind.

Exactly then, what is Black unity? Are White people unified? I believe the overwhelming majority of us would answer the second question with a thunderous affirmative and, with lightning speed. But any division or dispute that inspires us to say Black people are not unified can be found in the White community. Don't they quarrel on a great number of issues? Aren't they Protestants and Catholics, Republicans and Democrats (Black Americans are more unified when it comes to political parties). Some were against the war in Iraq while others think invading that country was a colossal mistake.

They seem to be split down the middle when it comes to the issue of Abortion. They fight each other at big league and little league baseball games. So what is it about us that makes us disunited?

If there really is a significant difference in Black and White unity it has to be in how and with whom we spend our money. It has been estimated that as much as 95 percent of the dollars spent by Black Americans are spent with other than Black owned businesses. However close this is to the truth, its cause should be called by the name "self-hate", if anything, and not "disunity" so we can zero in on what is wrong. Besides, when black people open viable, competitive business and do not win the support of black consumers, it may not be as much selective neglect inspired by self-hate as it is the absence conscious pro-black spending born of black self-love.

I believe with all my heart and soul that we are as unified physically as any other group but we are not unified *enough* to effectively solve the problems that plague us as a people. Perhaps this is what we have meant to say all along while giving it too broad of a name (disunity). But our intra-racial economic support cannot stop at merely rivaling White intra-racial economic support since their level of economic unity derives from no special efforts at selective intra-racial buying but rater the mere absence of any self-hate sentiments as we have in the black community.

Those who are lukewarm or colder to the black cause will not go out of their way or make the sacrifices, real or imaginary, to support Black business.

So am I saying Black disunity a myth? I believe it is

if you are talking about anything other than economics or saying whites too, are disunited.

If white people had to start today being 50 percent more loyal to the cause of White people than they already are, they too would struggle to make this happen and, failure to do so would inspire whites to say the type of things about "white disunity" that we say about Black disunity. We may very well be mislabeling a normal degree of variability "disunity" because we are predisposed to finding fault in things black people do.

Not only does the myth of Black disunity buttress the myth of black inferiority, but the popular, trigger-happy use of the word unity has curtailed many good minds from thinking our problems through and consequently acting to help bring about change. Enough of us must warm up to our cause. Too many of us are simply "default Americans" and chameleons.

Although I contend that we are no more disunited than White Americans, it stands to reason that they do not disrespect 'whiteness', as much as we as a group disrespect "blackness". But again, we simply cannot afford to just play catch up in this respect. As my brother once wrote, "The closer we come to catching up with White people, the farther behind we will get". I took this to mean that a target that focuses only on economic equality will distract us from the many non-material values that need our attention.

Indeed, we need to aim much higher than that. We need a high number of M spirits at the grassroots level and at least a sprinkling of them at all levels doing things such as extolling moral and intellectual the virtues of our ancestry as far back as we can see and pointing out the incredible things we do and have done in the contemporary world. To rid ourselves of our self-hate or self-disrespect we must show to ourselves how truly lovable and respectable we are, especially in a state of spiritual health. It just so happens we would not have to exaggerate.

As a matter of fact, we may need a shot of Ritalin as some of the things achieved by our ancestry seem just short of supernatural.

It might also be temptation for some of our sell-out "scholars" to join those voices who like to accuse Afrocentrists of inflated claims, not understanding that we have been hungry too long to take small bites out of the spiritual food we find in our spectacular past.

## CHAPTER XIII
## THE ISIS CRISIS

Those of us who care about future generations of Black people should always be mindful of inter-racial and intra-racial threats to our spiritual health. One of those threats, which I believe to be the most potent, comes from Eurocentric scholars, living and dead, mostly white, some black, who viciously protect the status quo without regard to truth, justice, or morality. In doing so they try to ensure that an edifice of white supremacy looms large enough for all black eyes to see and be discouraged from heterodox points of view.

The false Eurocentric ideas have contaminated

Hollywood and virtually all television production, two sources around which black and white world views are often built.

Yet we think Ku Klux Klansmen are the most threatening Negrophobes. Subduing them would only swat the gnat and permit the dragon to live. Those dragons are Eurocentric historians and their Hollywood henchmen.

If the Black collective is persuaded to believe that it is genetically doomed to inferiority, it will have to rely on the white collective to voluntarily repay its moral debt for the stolen goods it received. According to Fredrick Douglas, this will never happen. Besides, most of them will probably never see their inherited cultural and socioeconomic advantages as something stolen partially or fully.

To me it is irresponsible to forfeit any opportunity, big or small, to help spread the truth about our glorious and spectacular past.

White supremacy is an emotional intoxicant, which means no reference to "canons of evidence" can settle for Eurocentrists the disputes about who did what in the ancient world. If they are shown a smoking gun proving Afrocentric claims, the smoke only serves to make them high and cause them to respond with neurotic lies, such as the undeniable Negroid features of the Olmec Heads resulting from blunt tools used by Native Americans or the Black Madonnas of Europe having black skin because of candles and storms. I feel more than convinced that the Afrocentric "theory" of ancient Egypt is the correct one based on my own studies. But what would by itself, for me, have been good enough, is that Black scholars think so too. With that, I say, let's spread the good news.

## CHAPTER XIV
## I HAVE A NIGHTMARE

If I have not already done so in a previous chapter, I run the risk in this one of making readers think they are reading the words of a mad man. While that would put me in good historical company, I still prefer being thought of as being sane.

But since our struggle as a people is a million times more important than what people think of me, I shall proceed to challenge some seemingly self-evident notions and beliefs and attempt to illustrate that they are not based on sound reasoning at all. Even more important, they are very harmful to the recovery of our spiritual health. If I succeed, these arguments would reverberate throughout the Black community and shake the foundation of these fraudulent ideas, behind which the Malcolm Vacuums, the Unblacks, and the Samboites hide their cowardice, selfishness, and other excreta in their moral cesspools.

As it is, these "self-evident" beliefs stand tall on the stilts of faulty logic and wishful thinking. They are very inviting to the natural inertia of the human animal, particularly those looking for face-saving loopholes.

What sets great men and women apart from their mediocre contemporaries is their ability to escape the gravitational pull of such natural tendencies. If such inertial impulses are left unchecked and become too dominant in us, we will become easy prey for any predator with an appetite.


## Do Black Racists exist?

It was noticed a long time ago that some Black Americans had incorporated the same racist feelings toward Black people that White people often harbored. Of course, this book is about that very tendency, but the issue here is whether they can be racist toward White people. My answer to this is that they CAN be racist toward White people but they are NOT racist toward White people.

I say they *can* be racist toward white people only because there is recorded evidence that Black people of the ancient world regarded the white race as inferior. Therefore, if you wish to see a Black person who is racist toward white people, you missed your chance by several thousand years.

Modern Black people simply do not look down on White people on the basis of anything they consider hereditary, except maybe sports and dancing. Even this is kept in a light hearted vein and seems more amusing than offensive to all onlookers.

Notice I did not say that there are no Black people who are mad at the white race. If that makes them racist, I have no argument. But no white racist is just mad at the Black race and no dictionary definition of the word "racist" includes anger. Militant words or even deeds coming from Black individuals would, at best license us to call them "anti-white". Even then it is far more accurate to say the individual is anti-white supremacy. Unsophisticated minds sometimes make no distinction between the two. (One rapper says, "Black people ain't racist, they're just mad").

The "militant" Black individual's mind does not house the same thought patterns that inspire us to call an Adolph Hitler or a Bull Conner "racist". In fact, for every imaginary Black racist you show me, I will show you ten Black "anglophiles" (the best word I know to describe Black people who look up to the white race.) While the mindsets of the white supremacist and his imaginary Black counterpart share superficial similarities at best, their roots are radically different.

The Black "racist" sentiments do not come from a void. They don't hate white people because their skin is different or because their hair is different. Not only are Black people collectively tolerant to such differences, a great number of them, if not the majority, actually find white traits more desirable than their own.

The Black militant is always fire up about his interpretation of white-on-black racism. It is always based on vindictiveness, and is never wholly spontaneous.

The same can not be said of members of white supremacist groups.

I said all this to say that Black people rode in on the proverbial high horse and some whites are trying to steal a free ride by calling black people racist. We should not divest ourselves of the saddle by referring to each other as racist. By labeling each other with this ugly title, we help keep silent many would-be warriors and keep them from throwing remedial stones in the form of words, at ideas and problems that need to be stoned to death.

White people tend to embarrassed by their racist history and today's accusations. To save face, assuage guilt, and feel better about their racial selves, they naturally gravitate to the counterfeit logic of the Black "racist".

The white intellectual who pampers his less literate brethren by silence on or support for the black racist fallacy is dishonest , unmanly, or both.

None of us who are vocal about race-based problems in America or anywhere else should be handcuffed by fear of being labeled by a term that is much too nasty for the true contents of their hearts. Black America has ostracized and ignored too many great men by taking seriously the "racist" labels power brokers use to redirect us to the leadership of black wimps.

Finally, those who insist that there are modern-day black racists should find it strikingly odd that the word "Negrophobia" has no well-known interracial equivalent. Even more telling is the fact that the 21st edition of world book dictionary's definition of "racism" would eliminate virtually all the reasons the likes of Jessie Jackson, Al Sharpton and Louis Farrakhan get called racists by conservatives whites and unthinking black people..

The idea of a Black "racist" might spend the night in a good mind, but it will only find a happy home in a dull mind.

**Hate Is Amoral**

While I vehemently reject the idea that any black person today hates white people because they are white, I *do* believe that there are black people who are passionately angry at the white race for other reasons. What I *don't* believe is that "hate" belongs on anybody's moral scale. In other words, none of us will burn in Hell for hating nor will any of us thrive in Heaven for loving. Hate is however, very dangerous and less desirable than love. Hate is not "wrong" but rather an indication that something IS wrong. (I can almost hear a chorus of protesters as I write).

Both hate and love are involuntary responses to external stimuli which come in both personal and symbolic form. We simply cannot turn love or hate on and off at will. Even the biblical Solomon says there is a time to hate. The Bible also says that God hated Esau.

Those who contend that hate is wrong are forced to conclude that the wise King Solomon didn't know what he was talking about and worst yet, that the omniscient creator was wrong.

It is my firm belief that hate and fear are emotional twins bearing only different names. The existence of two different words may only be semantically useful.

I do not write for the purpose of defending hate or undermining love. What I aim to do is take a stab at the naive cheerleader mentality which assumes that we can cheer away hate or cheer love into existence. We can speak pretty words all day long but the problems will not go away until we field the right players who execute the right plays.

## Black Role Models

Middle class, college-educated black Americans, a large number of which I would classify as Unblacks, seem to be fond of whining about what they consider the lack of role models in the Black community. I get the feeling that this group, deep down inside, knowing that it doesn't have a clue, is just trying to sound pretentiously wise or they are reaching for easy, pre-packaged answers.

What bothers me is that the words of this recurring complaint is usually their closing statement which tends to close their minds and those nearby to the need for a real and perhaps more challenging solution.

Such whiners probably assume whites and other groups have "enough" role models. If they do have enough, they did not manufacture them, which is what the whiners are suggesting we need to do somehow. The quantitative sufficiency of role models is nothing more than a corollary aspect of spiritual health, which is in turn nothing more than the absence of a spiritual disease like our Sambo virus.

If we miraculously found "enough" black role models with which to flood Black America, we would simultaneously have access to a spiritually healthy general black pool. This is like saying the secret to a sixty year marriage is to make it to the 59th anniversary.

However, it might be a good idea to devise programs which amplify model behavior.

## Is Black History Irrelevant?

If you, dear reader, trust anything I have written, please trust this: No one cares more about our present and our future than the ones who study and record our past. The book of Isaiah states that "to see the future you must look backwards".

It baffles me that some people don't see what appears to me plain as the fleshy nose on their face: the need for Black people to know their true history.

Voltaire said that those who don't know history are doomed to repeat it. While I think he was right, that is not my complaint. Those who would have us "come out of the past" are asking us to forfeit the best testimonials against the questions surrounding our collective human worth.

Although I am not without admiration about some of the achievements of other groups, I would not trade our history before the slave trade for any other two combined.

Evidently the black naysayers of Black history, assuming they care at all, tend to favor only concrete answers and approaches to our problems, such as government-sponsored programs. (I would favor them too If I thought they were efficacious.) Perhaps they fail to fathom how knowing what Black people accomplished in the BC world or anytime earlier than the nightly news, can have any meaningful impact on our lives today.

It has occurred to me that their minds are unable to square a "tribal" Africa with the claims of a spectacular past. (I call this the Hut/Tut Paradox). There is no doubt in my mind whatsoever that what is recorded and propagated about the ancient Greeks has inspired several generations of European thinkers and innovators which helped bring them and their descendants to their current level of comfort.

We need to know our history because we need to believe in ourselves, not just as individuals, but in the black family as a whole. We need more than any group in history, to know our history.

White people did not get to their comfort zone because they know their history but because they did not have to contend with "His-story" (a term meaning the false Eurocentric version of Black and White history).

Our history tells us about our possibilities, and it helps offset the multifarious suggestions to the contrary. Far too many of us consciously and unconsciously think that black people are inherently defective. This affects how we raise our children and how we regard our neighbors, among other things.

I am not claiming that history is the only thing that can make black self-love and self-respect happen, but that it is currently the only one that has clearly taken shape in my mind. I used to tell my children that black history is more of a vitamin than it is a medicine.

I am thoroughly convinced that when we learn and crystallize who we really are, virtually all desiderata will fall in place.

# CHAPTER XV
## I LOVE BLACK PEOPLE WHO LOVE BLACK PEOPLE

A beautiful young girl who was helping her grandmother with the catering of our biannual family reunion tried unsuccessfully from the kitchen about sixty feet away to pick up on the theme of a play staged for the occasion.

Shortly after the play was over I walked into the kitchen for a reason I fail to recall. But I do remember her asking me when I reached that destination what the play was about. I explained that it was a reenactment of some of the more memorable times and experiences of my wife's family history. When I told her that the narrative that was being read along with the scenes touched on Black History in general, her big bright eyes seemed to sparkle as she gasped slightly, implying that that is what she thought she was hearing. She was obviously pleasantly surprised and therefore anxiously told me of her plans to study Black History at the collegiate level. I too was pleasantly surprised somewhat to learn that a 15 year old in this part of the world nowadays would be *that* interested in the subject.

In the course of conversing with her for about fifteen minutes, I told her about the Olmec Heads and what they implied. Without any sign of an unwarranted pessimism or disinterest, she told me that she wanted to see these things for herself. With a fresh secondary education curing in her efficient brain, she immediately understood how the Olmec Heads would upset orthodox accounts of written history.

All the while we talked, she looked me squarely in the eyes, expressing herself with the kind of confidence that comes not from the presence of pride but the utter absence of self-doubt. When I discovered who her grandmother was, a very likable, unpretentious woman with whom I was already acquainted, the young lady's personality fit easily with what I would have expected.

Virtually everything else I heard and saw that night before and after my encounter with this angel, I have forgotten. That brief moment talking to her filled my heart with delight and mellowed me for several days.

Her sweet, thoughtful attitude toward black people and their struggle and her radiant personality in general will never leave my memory bank.

She also poured a cup of hope in my mind that maybe there are enough M Spirits to rescue us from the hideous monster whose fangs have only yet snagged our britches, compared to the bigger bite that will come unless we act appropriately.

The full hope of our recovery rests with none other than people like her who have pre-legree thought patterns and at least a small measure of the M-spirit.

This is one of the main reasons why I love Black people who love Black people.

Although I like and dislike people for other reasons, my love, hate and all in between tends to be based on their attitude toward the struggle. I am thoroughly convinced that M-spirits are direct deposits of the cosmic will, which roughly corresponds in my mind to the Judeo-Christian conception of God.

I suspect that throughout the history of mankind, high concentrations of that *will* have been placed in a select few humans. Some of them achieved great fame while others died in obscurity, operating in small circles, but still helping to change the world.

I feel myself very fortunate to have in my own personal circle several individuals who whose Afrocentric spirit is not rooted in spite but rather enlightenment and love. All of them are exceedingly intelligent and well-rounded in other aspects of their lives.

I sometimes hate to look up and see one of them

coming because they are so interesting for me to talk to and I can never resist engaging in marathon conversations with them. They galvanize my thoughts sometimes and cause me to forget or neglect appointments and otherwise small obligations.

So often do they tell me horror stories of the kind chronicled in chapter eight?

Of course I don't like the idea of the stress they often endure, but it is sometimes good to know that they too detest the anti-black things they hear coming out of the mouths of black faces.

"Some of us lost our heads coming to America on the slave ships", lamented one of the aforementioned Afrocentrists. Lucky for us some black people never left the continent of Africa spiritually.

# CHAPTER XVI
## AN UNORGANIZED ARMY

There is no material solution to our problems. All the money in the world will not make them go away. There is no quick fix for the self-hate and self-doubt that undermine our powers to solve these problems. There are no slick short cuts. Slogans will not lead to self love and confidence. Neither can they be willed into existence. They must fall in place, which will happen only after the cesspool of false ideas about blackness have been banished from our brains and we realize the true worth of the children of Africa.

The real difficulty in solving our problems lies not in

figuring out *what* needs to be done, but rather in the weakness of the *will* to do what needs to be done.

When that will becomes great enough we will act and reason without blind respect to convention, received wisdom, the need for acceptance, or even possibly physical danger.

What we need is an army of individuals working in their own personal circles, acting against self-hate, self doubt, both of which cripple the giant step toward redemption. I believe that army is already afoot, although scattered and unorganized, and it should stay that way. What is missing in many of these plain-clothes warriors is a keen sense of mission. It is my guess that most of them have yet to engage in any real battle, doing only that which is incidental to their own personal frustrations and provocative encounters with black expressions of anti-blackness and other issues.

This would make them more reactive than pro-active when it comes to using their divine endowments to change anti-black thought patterns. They know or almost know that we are at war with a set of intra-racial mindsets that need to be defeated. Their wills, which I believe to be part of the divine will, are weakened by a sense of loneliness and by contemplation of the sheer size of the fight that needs to be fought.

There was a time in my life when I was more intellectually than existentially interested in the Black struggle. But over the years I have come to realize that we are in big trouble. The people I love most are in danger. That danger may even be mortal on a scale much bigger than the one we already know causing black on black homicide and disease. The responsibility to change our sorry condition and this sorry world is yours and mine, dear reader. No matter how guilty anybody is on the outside, it is ours and ours alone.

As far as I am concerned, the expected messiah has already done his job. As my brother-in-law aptly put it "Jesus left us a pattern to live by". If you ask me enough of us emulating the one they called the Nazarene (not the Jesus of ecclesiolatry) becomes then the blueprint for rebuilding the people who built the pyramids.

The famous anthropologist, Margaret Mead is quoted as having said "Never doubt that a few thoughtful and committed people can change the world". I am hoping that if this work does nothing else, it helps strengthen the will of those the divine will has genetically scheduled to help put a people back on course.

I do not need to give you my brothers and sisters, a set of instructions on what to do and how to do it. I would only have you increase the pro-black things you already do and say and encourage like spirits to do the same. In case my own style might stimulate some ideas in formulating your approach, I will cite some examples for you to consider. These things are not the result of profound inspiration but rather expressions of my love for black people as a group and good old fashioned trial and error.

Every chance I get, I smile and interact with a black child, often letting it be known that I think he or she is beautiful and intelligent. I never have to put on an act, although if I did it would not be a bad thing. To me this is pro-black although I try not to label it as such unless it is applicable to my point or objective.

I un-spitefully try to avoid using popular quintessential terms such as "another Einstein" or "it doesn't take a rocket scientist...". This may seem petty or small to some but these things add up.

I talk ad nauseam about the greatness of ancient Africa. Sometimes I am pleasantly surprised at how receptive and hungry people are to hear such things.

I make it a point not to criticize black leaders who are fighting for justice no matter what tactics they use. I don't care what motivates them.

As tactfully as I can, I speak against ecclesiolatry and that "form of Godliness"seemingly foretold in the Pauline Epistles. Many Christian churches seem to have taken man's relationship to man out of the equation, which seems to me the main theme of Jesus' ministry. I think it borders on criminal to nurse the illusion that mankind can measure God's will with micro-specificity.

I sometimes bubble with enthusiasm relating success stories like Marva Collins', a Chicago educator who worked wonders with Black students wrongly labeled by the public school system. Such stories speak volumes on the unsung and sometimes inhibited powers of the Black mind. I use the stories over and over as "head bread" to feed those who are hungry for a sense of wholeness.

I patronize Black-owned business and I brag to the world about the quality of the goods or service thusly received. Again, I don't have to put on an act.

These are just some of the things I do or have done with a sense of duty that derives from my love.

We must work like this to enshrine a set of communal values that encompass education, economics, and psychology at the very least.

Let no one satisfy us saying we need to work together like Korean-Americans, Jewish Americans, or any other group. Our communal values must have a much greater intensity and cohesiveness than the best of these. We must become the envy of the ants and the bees.

This is why what we do in our personal circles is so important.

You need not go atop Mount Olive to enumerate beatitudes or the Lincoln Memorial to talk about a dream. You need only to shine in your sphere of movement.

At the very least you should feel compelled to respond to any suggestion or commentary which even remotely suggest that Black people are in any way genetically inferior. Take comfort, my brothers and sisters, in the fact that there are others like you nearby and in the distance, afraid, lonely, and in need of spiritual camaraderie. Find them. Befriend them. Gather together with them to exchange freely and recharge each other's spirit. Let the spiritual recovery of our people be a new gospel and spread it with missionary zeal.

Curse me, if you wish, for any pain you might experience doing what you were programmed to do before the big bang.

Be like some people I am fortunate to know: wear your afrocentricity with a dignity which almost by itself proclaims counterfeit any other ism.

Stand up to ecclesiolatry and advertise without spite your love for black people in general.

## CHAPTER XVII
## CONCLUSION

Has any other group in all history been more misguided than the people who inspired this book. At the very least they are among the hoodwinked elite when considering the incomprehensible gap of truth and logic between being the first race to be thought of as superior and the race being looked down on the most. Is evolution that fast or clumsy?

The problem these poor deluded souls represent is ours and ours alone. They do not pose a threat to another racial or ethnic group. Why would anybody else particularly want them to go away? It is our duty to clean up the mess they are and the mess they help make.

We must proselytize as many Malcolm Vacuums as possible into a new level of consciousness. We must, if necessary, shame the Unblack into doing better. We must send the incorrigible Samboite into hiding.

If I thought their thoughts were inconsequential and not in the way of our ability to solve our own problems, I would not say another word on the issue for the rest of my life. I could certainly use a break from the emotional pain my values often bring.

But since I believe neutralization of the thoughts they air by words, deeds and dereliction would be a tremendous leap forward for us, I will not change my ways. I am hoping that many of us will continue to adopt at least a similar point of view. We cannot afford to be 40 million races of one in America.

Yes, of course, we must attend to the affairs in our own personal backyards but we must bear in mind that we live in a village of blackness no matter our place of residency. Our lives are inextricably interwoven.

We must therefore clearly define and enshrine a set of values that are essentially healthy for our recovery, even if not pro-black by name. We must also clearly define a set of anti-black sins and work against the easy atmosphere that permits black verbal transgressions against our sense of worth.

I want to be loved by everybody and so do you, dear reader, but if we must be like the Green Hornet, a fictional crime fighter who everybody thought was a criminal, then so be it. When the Samboites, Malcolm Vacuums, and Unblacks air their brain-dead ideas in my presence, I try my best to respond with lightning bolts of contradictory opinions. I consider it my moral duty to do so. I'm not sure whether it is right to respond with tact, rage, or something in between, but I am perfectly sure, as I said earlier, that silence is always wrong.

If the thought patterns of these sick individuals were harmless, silence might be the best response. But how black people feel about the Black race is connected to everything in our lives, good and bad. It determines whether we open private schools to get the job done or sit quietly by and allow incompetent school systems throw academic nuts and bolts at our children with an assembly line mentality.

How black people feel about Black people affects parent-child relationships. It affects boy-girl relations.

We must change how we feel about blackness for the better and thereby free ourselves for the first time in four hundred years. Our enslavement began not when they stole our bodies from Africa but when we began to despise and disown Africa and everything African, including ourselves.

Voodoo is automatically evil and bad. Mumbo Jumbo, an African deity, is a term for something unintelligible or meaningless.

Where are the pure thinkers who realize we are simply seeing the glass labeled "European" as half-full while seeing the African glass containing the same amount of water as half empty?

If we would just wake up and begin to ask questions, we will follow a trail of answers that lead to where I am right now.

In my mind Africa nor any of its children owes nobody an apology except maybe those long-dead Europeans it held in servitude in ancient Nubia and Egypt.

The Africa in my mind is something to embrace and thank God every day that it is my heritage and not somebody else's. My Africa is something to draw strength from, not to run from.

My Africa inspires wonder in my soul and lets me know there is something special in us and that there is more to reality than meets the academic or "scientific" eye.

Finally I want to say, my dearly departed mother would not approve of my declaration of hate for anybody. I would only hope that she would understand that I never set out to do so and that if I could cease feeling the way I feel, I would in a heartbeat. I don't like it at all, but I know it is traceable to my love for the people that I love.

Then there are others who will no doubt think that the subject of this book should not be out in the open and I can't say that I blame them. But out in the open is the only place it can get the fresh air that it needs. This subjects it to the purifying effects of those who might examine it closer, diagnose it better, and apply antiseptic strategies.

I do not see this phenomenon as the measles. I see it as a cancer. Remission would mean some wonderful things for Black America and the rest of the world. Therefore, I say it again in closing. I hate Black people who hate Black people. The realization of the existence of a force more potent and abhorrent than white supremacy stands no chance of inspiring any other emotion in my soul. I love you, my brothers and sisters.

## CHAPTER XVIII
## THE DICTIONARY OF BLACK LOGIC

The Sambo Virus is defined as a sickness of the human spirit that afflicts people of African descent throughout the world. It is characterized mainly by paradoxical thought patterns in which Black people hold the Black race in low esteem and practice a silent form of intra-racial bigotry.

The Sambo Virus originated in the sixteenth century as Africans were subjected to raw, unabashed expressions of racial hatred, which, conspired with their separation from their cultures, and eventually led them to devalue their own human worth as their memory of the great cultures of the motherland faded.

Examples of spiritual diseases and disorders associated with the Sambo Virus include self/group hatred, self-doubt, overweening respect or admiration for people of European descent, material-based measurements of self-worth, and religious hypocrisy.

The following glossary introduces a set of words and phrases whose popularization might help sensitize us to some of the more harmful of these maladies or thought patterns, and possibly help move us closer to a healthier spiritual outlook.

The terms and definitions included in this glossary are intended to help spotlight and label our spiritual diseases and other thought patterns related to our struggle. The general idea is to inject our everyday language with easy-to-remember terms whose catchiness and relevance induce people to use them frequently in casual and formal exchange. In doing so, they will help disarm these spiritual diseases and disorders of their invisibility. The aim is to make such patterns of thought easier targets for pro-black opposition and other hygienic responses.

At a certain level of popularity the names/terms assigned to these thought patterns would act as mirrors in which we see our spiritual sickness with greater clarity.

As it is these patterns of thought array themselves in mindsets, beliefs, dispositions, opinions, perspectives, values, etc. They enjoy an anonymity which makes them considerably more toxic and formidable than they would be attached to a popular name.

Ideally, every such pattern of thought or spiritual disease that can rightly be defined as anti-black or harmful to our cause should be captured by a special name/term. Consciousness of these names/terms will, among other things, help us catch ourselves before thoughtlessly speaking or acting against our own spiritual health. Arthur Schopenhauer, a famous philosopher, appears to have seen the value of attaching names to certain thought patterns as he wrote: "It would be a very good thing if every trick could receive some short and obviously appropriate name, so that when a man used this or that particular trick, he could at once be reproved for it".

While these patterns of thought are not tricks in the sense intended by Schopenhauer, many of them do bear a conceptual slipperiness that a spicy name would help crystallize.

Most of the newly-coined words and phrases included in this collection have been constructed with the use of literary devices such as rhymes, puns, etc. in an attempt to make them catchy and exotic sounding, thereby sticking better to the memory.

**Abstract Black** Mentally committed to Afrocentrism or pro-blackness but not realistically focused on things that tend to offset the effects of white supremacy. 2. A Black person who is preoccupied by symbols of pro-blackness while disinterested in the real aspects of the struggle.

**Afropo** Adj. (Something or someone) resistant to or tending to be resistant to white supremacy or its false assumptions 2. Favorable to the progress of the Black struggle. 3. Having the potential to improve black self-respect. 3. Appropriate for presentation to impressionable black minds. (pun/hybrid of apropos and Afro).

**Aim-nesia** A mind-set in which the focus is on the organization, institution, program, means, etc. itself rather than the purpose for which it was created. 2. Under-emphasis or neglect of a goal, aim, or purpose of something. 3. Forgetting the aim or purpose of something. (hybrid of "aim" and "amnesia").

**The Back Door Complex** The tendency of some Black people, as a result of miseducation, to: a) stubbornly resist ideas, facts, and opinions that support the concept of Black equality/worth b) blindly expect the worst from other Black people and even imagine evidence of Black inferiority where there is none.

**Belliver** one who believes, but professes otherwise, that IQ scores truly represent the innate abilities of individuals and races. (hybrid of Bell, short for Bell curve, and Believer)

**Blackbone** The courage and/or conviction to speak up for or champion a cause of Black people. (hybrid of

BLACK and BACKBONE).

**Blackteria** 1.Any Black person whose mind houses false or harmful ideas about the black race. 2. Malcolm Vacuums, Unblacks, and Samboites as a group or the harmful things they say and do. (hybrid of Black and Bacteria).

**'Bout Out** A student who is at risk of becoming a school drop out but is still amenable to staying in school with the right emotional support.

**Caesar Pleaser** A black person who says and does things which he/she knows or estimates will be met with popular approval by Whites or white power brokers. 2. Something said or done to achieve this end.

**Celebrity Blindness** A mindset wherein a Black person, due to his/her celebrity status or popularity (e.g. actor, star athlete, etc.), feels him/herself fully accepted or valued by Whites and is therefore unable or unwilling to objectively evaluate or recognize racism or ethnocentrism in many instances.

**Collins Gap** The gap between the actual academic performance of Black students collectively and the potential academic performance with effective pedagogic approaches. (named for Marva Collins)

**The Crab Complex** A state of mind in which people

are given to envy and jealousy, which inspires them to do and say things which obstruct or tend to obstruct the progress of other people. (Jawanza Kunjufu used this term in his book "Black Economics").

**Ebony Ebb** The general weakening of the Black race or the increase in its vulnerability to racial injustice as signified by disorders such as high rates of incarceration, high percentage of children born to single mothers, high rate of school drop outs, intra-racial violence, famine, and disease.

**Ego-nomics** The practice of seeking to acquire money and material things in order to project one's self as prosperous, important, respectable, etc. 2 Equating self-worth with net worth. (Hybrid of EGO and ECONOMICS)

**Foe-Phobia** - A mind-set in which one fears being opposed, disliked, unpopular, etc. or fears doing and saying things he or she knows to be right but will or may be met with popular disapproval.

**The Fourth R** Academic reinforcement provided by parents or guardians by making sure that the student studies properly, does his/her homework, understands the lessons, and behaves appropriately in school. (spin-off of "The three r's")

**Gnosis Amaurosis** A mind-set in which one is not aware of one's own ignorance. 2. A state of mind in which one does not know that one does not know. (Gnosis=knowledge + amaurosis, a form of blindness).

**The God Façade** An outward appearance of righteousness, holiness, piety, etc. which belies an attitude of selfishness, greed, envy, dishonesty, immorality, etc.

**Head Bread** Anything, a fact, historical or present-day, a study, an experiment, etc. which has the potential to increase Black confidence in Black intelligence or any other virtue.

**Hid-Story** Historical truth that is not widely known. 2. A hidden or omitted fact or truth. 3. Historical truth that is not recorded in most history books. (pun of HID and HISTORY).

**His-Story** (traditional term) The Eurocentric story or version of history, which many Black people see as distorted, falsified, etc. in order to inflate the image of the white race.

**The High Tech Effect** An effect in which Black people attribute superior intelligence to the White race after marveling at "their" technological achievements such as facsimile machines, VCRs, Microwaves, etc., while being oblivious to the contributions Black intelligence may have made to the technology in the form of direct creative input or laying the theoretical groundwork in ancient or medieval Africa.

**The Hut-Tut Paradox** 1. The seeming irreconcilability of a modern-day "primitive" Africa with the extraordinary facts of Black Africa's cultural/technological past. 2. The difficulty for some, especially those with limited knowledge of Africa, to believe or take seriously claims about Black Africa's historical greatness, inasmuch as they often harbor preconceived notions of a tribal, barbaric Africa. 3. The inability to reconcile one's false image of Africa and Africans with the fact that Black people built the world's first civilizations.

**Id Kid** A child who is growing up in a very permissive environment, or household where there is little or no emphasis on right and wrong. 2. A child who receives poor or substandard parental guidance and support. According to Freudian psychology, the "id", one of the three parts of the human personality, is characterized by unrestrained pleasure-seeking impulses. It is irrational and selfish. The "id" is normally checked by the "ego" and the "superego". The "superego" is the seat of one's moral attitude. Thus "id kid" is meant to define a child whose superego is underdeveloped, meaning the child's personality is dominated by instinctive drives.

**I.Q. Icon** A well-known person who is seen as a towering intellect (usually historical). 2. One reputed to possess great mental abilities, such as Einstein,

Socrates, etc.

**Ishakamusa Shock** A method of countering the overweening, unwarranted awe, respect, etc. that some Black people feel toward whites as a race or white power, which includes pointing out or pointing to some of the more unflattering aspects of their history and culture. (Inspired by the writer, Rev. Dr. Ishakamusa Barishango, whose books "African People and European Holidays: A mental Genocide" Books I, II, III, reports many such facts and information).

**The Isis Crisis** The crisis of the denial of the Blackness of the ancient Egyptians by Eurocentric scholars and their tendency to undermine evidence such as that supporting the contention that the Americas were visited by Africans centuries before Columbus was born (named for the Egyptian goddess, Isis).

**Kaleidoscope hope** The desire, movement, goal, etc. for Blacks, Whites and all races to live together in harmony and equality.

**Kemet Chemistry** How black people relate to Black people. 2. How Black people feel about other black people. 3. The strength of Black love for Black people in general. (Kemet is the ancient name for Egypt).

**Madhubuti Duty** The moral obligations of Black

individuals with special insights, advantages, abilities, etc., to help other less fortunate Black people. (inspired by views express by Haki R. Madhubuti in his book "Black Men: Obsolete, Single, Dangerous).

**Malcolm Vacuum** A Black individual, family, community, etc. in which there is little or no awareness of or concern for the issues, values, etc. related to the Black struggle. 2. A person who is not aware of the intellectual resistance, (historiography, IQ testing, Eurocentrism, etc.) of White supremacy. (Named for Malcolm X).

**Maltruism** The absence of concern for the welfare or well-being of others. 2. The opposite of altruism.

**Mama Trauma** The negative things parents, guardians or other close relatives do and say to their very young children that damage or tend to impair their emotional development, especially confidence.

**Mayflower Power** The inherited advantages (material and emotional) that modern whites enjoy because of their ancestor's enslavement and exploitation of Black people. (The Mayflower was the ship that brought the first pilgrims to America. "Mayflower Power" is intended to denote the advantage of being the descendant of immigrants over being the descendant of slaves).

**Mis-education** (traditional term) The process during

which Black people learn things such as working for and managing businesses, enterprises, etc. outside the Black community versus starting their own business, to neglect Black owned businesses, or to think of Black people as hopelessly inferior.

**Moongazer** A Black person who has overweening admiration for white people.

**The M Spirit** Strong proactive will to overcome or resist the effects of racial injustice, Eurocentrism or any other threat to the short or long range welfare of Black people. 2. Concern or anxiety related to the condition of Black people. 3. One who possesses the "M" Spirit. I call them M Spirits because there seems to be a noticeably high frequency of outstanding Black leaders, innovators, groups, etc. whose first or last name begins with the letter M. For example, Martin Luther King, Marcus Garvey, Marva Collins, Nelson Mandela, Melanin, Malcolm X, Mali, Maroons, Mandingo, etc.

**Okkk** Adj. Tending to favor white supremacy. 2. Harmful to Black people or their progress. (pun/hybrid of OK and KKK).

**The Omni School** Everything, including non-academic factors such as self image, parent involvement, teacher expectation, student motivation, etc. that effects a student's academic performance.

**Ought to Eight** The period of child development (between zero and eight years of age), during which a high percentage of the personality foundation is believed to establish itself.

**The Pigment Figment** The imagined natural superiority of Whites or the false belief in Black inferiority.

**Pot-kettle Prejudice** Black prejudice against other Black people.

**Pre-Legree** (as a Black person) Free of self-hate, race-based self-doubt or having no doubt about the equality of Black intelligence. 2. Before the time when Black people were enslaved and subjected to the dehumanizing effects of racial injustice. 3. To become free of self-hate, self-doubt. (named for Simon Legree, the cruel overseer in Harriet Beecher Stowe's novel, "Uncle tom's Cabin").

**Pygmalion Effect** (traditional term) An effect in which a teacher's expectations influence a student's academic performance.

**Reverse Race Card** A strategic device in which a White individual accuses a Black person of playing the race card or unnecessarily labeling something "racist". 2. An unwarranted accusation of "playing the race card" 3. An unwarranted accusation, by whites, of "reverse racism".

**Sambo Virus**, the A paradoxical pattern of thoughts wherein Black people themselves hold the Black race in low esteem and practice a silent form of intraracial bigotry.

**The School Of Self Hatred** All of the things in the society which teach or contribute to Black self-hatred, self-doubt, etc. such as unrepresentative images of Africa, African culture, Eurocentric historiography, religious images portrayed in non black images, popular myths and stereotypes, Eurocentric standards of beauty, and the suggestive influence of racist actions.

**Self Deaf** 1. As a black person, having a mind-set that is characterized by indifference, being lukewarm, hostile or pessimistic toward anything related to the moral, spiritual, or economic redemption of Black people. 2. Insensitive, as a Black person, to racial injustice affecting other Black people.

**Shoot the Sphinx** To deny, reject, undermine, or distort a well-documented or reasonably believable fact of Black or African History. 2 .to try to hide, cover up, distort, etc. a fact, historical truth, success story, etc. which might cast the Black race in a positive light. (Inspired by the disputed story that Napoleon and his army, upon seeing the face of the sphinx monument, shot its nose because of its Africoid features).

**Soul Tax** A voluntary sacrifice in which one does things such as pay higher than average prices for goods and services or gives up some other advantage, convenience, etc. in order to patronize a Black-owned business. 2. Any sacrifice to help black people.

**Samboite** A Black person who has an extremely low opinion of and looks down on the Black races as a whole. 2. A Black person who hates Black people.

**Samboism** The practice or belief in which Black people hate or look down on the Black race.

**Tomtation** Anything that tends to tempt Black people to compromise their loyalty to the Black community. 2. Any method, means, etc. used by Whites to exploit Black people for their own advantage. 3. The pressure on Black people to do and say things they think will please White people or meet with their approval (Hybrid of Tom and Temptation).

**The Trail to Jail** The social conditions, experiences, etc. which tend to lead to a life of crime or antisocial behavior, maladjustments, etc. (examples: substandard parenting, poverty, low self esteem, self hate, white racism, family dysfunction, verbal abuse, etc.).

**Unblack** A black person who has little to know interest in issues related to the black struggle.

**Utopia Myopia** A narrow-minded point of view in which one stubbornly maintains or defends utopian or idealistic values despite the fact that they are neither practical nor prudent or even logically tenable in a certain context.

**Woodsonian** Anything that encourages or inspires Black people to do things such as support and start Black businesses, admire the greatness of Africa's past, and not blindly imitate others in religion, education, etc. (named for Dr. Carter G. Woodson).